First World War
and Army of Occupation
War Diary
France, Belgium and Germany

29 DIVISION
Divisional Troops
Royal Army Service Corps
Divisional Train (225, 226, 227, 228 Companies A.S.C.)
20 March 1916 - 31 October 1919

WO95/2297/4

The Naval & Military Press Ltd
www.nmarchive.com
Published in association with The National Archives

Published by

The Naval & Military Press Ltd

Unit 10 Ridgewood Industrial Park,

Uckfield, East Sussex,

TN22 5QE England

Tel: +44 (0) 1825 749494

www.naval-military-press.com

www.nmarchive.com

This diary has been reprinted in facsimile from the original. Any imperfections are inevitably reproduced and the quality may fall short of modern type and cartographic standards.

© Crown Copyright
Images reproduced by permission of The National Archives, London, England, 2015.

Contents

Document type	Place/Title	Date From	Date To
Heading	WO95/2297-4		
Heading	29th Division Divl Troops 29th Divl Train A.S.C. Mar 1916-Oct 1919 225-226 Coy ASC To Independent Div		
Heading	Historical Account of 29th Divisional Train (225 to 228 Companies A.F.B)		
Miscellaneous	Historical Account of The 29th Divisional Train.		
Miscellaneous	Honours & Awards		
War Diary	Left England	20/03/1916	20/03/1916
War Diary	Havre	21/03/1916	23/03/1916
War Diary	Ailly	24/03/1916	31/03/1916
War Diary	Left England.	20/03/1916	20/03/1916
War Diary	Havre	21/03/1916	23/03/1916
War Diary	Ailly	24/03/1916	31/03/1916
War Diary	Le Havre	21/03/1916	21/03/1916
War Diary	Served	21/03/1916	24/03/1916
War Diary	Ailly Le Haut Clocher	24/03/1916	25/03/1916
War Diary	Famechon	25/03/1916	31/03/1916
Heading	War Diary of No 4 Coy 29th Divl Train A.S.C. from April 1st-1916 to April 30th 1916 Volume 2		
War Diary	Beauquesne.	01/04/1916	03/04/1916
War Diary	Raincheval.	04/04/1916	13/04/1916
War Diary	Louvencourt.	14/04/1916	30/04/1916
War Diary	Famechon	01/04/1916	04/04/1916
War Diary	Raincheval	04/04/1916	14/04/1916
War Diary	Louvencourt	14/04/1916	26/04/1916
War Diary	Arqueves	27/04/1916	30/05/1916
Heading	War Diary of 29th Divisional Train A.S.C. From July 1st 1916 To July 31st 1916 (Volume 5.)		
War Diary	Arqueves	01/07/1916	20/07/1916
War Diary	In Camp Near Vauchelles	21/07/1916	28/07/1916
War Diary	Poperinghe	29/07/1916	01/08/1916
War Diary	Proven Road.	02/08/1916	31/08/1916
Heading	War Diary of 29th Divisional Train A.S.C. From September 1st 1916 to September 30th 1916. (Volume 7)		
War Diary	Proven Road.	01/09/1916	30/09/1916
Heading	War Diary Of 29th Divisional Train A.S.C. From October 1st 1916 To October 31st 1916 (Volume 8.)		
War Diary	Proven Road.	01/10/1916	06/10/1916
War Diary	Travelling.	07/10/1916	07/10/1916
War Diary	Corbie.	08/10/1916	09/10/1916
War Diary	Ribemont.	10/10/1916	18/10/1916
War Diary	E.10. Central.	19/10/1916	31/10/1916
Heading	War Diary of 29th Divisional Train A.S.C. From November 1st 1916 to November 30th 1916. (Volume 9.)		
War Diary	Corbie.	01/11/1916	15/11/1916
War Diary	Treux.	16/11/1916	16/11/1916
War Diary	A. 15 C.	17/11/1916	30/11/1916

Heading	War Diary of 29th Divisional Train A.S.C. From December 1st 1916 to December 31st 1916. (Volume 10.)		
War Diary	A. 15 C.	01/12/1916	11/12/1916
War Diary	Corbie.	12/12/1916	13/12/1916
War Diary	Oissy.	14/12/1916	31/12/1916
Heading	War Diary Of 29th Divisional Train A.S.C. From January 1st 1917 to January 31st 1917. (Volume II.)		
War Diary	Oissy.	01/01/1917	10/01/1917
War Diary	Corbie.	11/01/1917	14/01/1917
War Diary	A. 15. C.	15/01/1917	31/01/1917
Heading	War Diary of 29th Divisional Train A.S.C. From February 1st to February 28th. 1917 (Volume 12)		
War Diary	A.15 C.	01/02/1917	07/02/1917
War Diary	Heilly.	08/02/1917	19/02/1917
War Diary	Minden Post.	20/02/1917	28/02/1917
Heading	War Diary of 29th Divisional Train A.S.C. From March 1st. to March 31st. 1917 (Volume 13)		
War Diary	Minden Post.	01/03/1917	03/03/1917
War Diary	Heilly.	04/03/1917	18/03/1917
War Diary	Oissy.	19/03/1917	28/03/1917
War Diary	Vignacourt.	29/03/1917	30/03/1917
War Diary	Beauval.	31/03/1917	31/03/1917
Heading	War Diary of 29th Divisional Train A.S.C. From April 1st. To April 31st. 1917 (Volume 14)		
War Diary	Beauval	01/04/1917	04/04/1917
War Diary	Bavincourt.	05/04/1917	11/04/1917
War Diary	Agnez	12/04/1917	12/04/1917
War Diary	Dainville	13/04/1917	13/04/1917
War Diary	Arras	14/04/1917	23/04/1917
War Diary	Berneville	24/04/1917	24/04/1917
War Diary	Wanquetin.	25/04/1917	25/04/1917
War Diary	Couin.	26/04/1917	30/04/1917
Heading	War Diary Of 29th Divisional Train A.S.C. From May, 1st, To May, 31st., 1917. (Volume 15)		
War Diary	Couin.	01/05/1917	01/05/1917
War Diary	Arras.	02/05/1917	08/05/1917
War Diary	Berneville.	09/05/1917	14/05/1917
War Diary	Arras.	15/05/1917	31/05/1917
Heading	War Diary of 29th Divisional Train A.S.C. From 1st. June, 1917 To 30th. June, 1917. (Volume 16.)		
War Diary	Arras.	01/06/1917	03/06/1917
War Diary	Lucheux	04/06/1917	04/06/1917
War Diary	Bernaville	05/06/1917	26/06/1917
War Diary	Proven	27/06/1917	29/06/1917
War Diary	International Corner.	30/06/1917	30/06/1917
Heading	War Diary of 29th. Divisional Train, A.S.C. From, 1st. July. 1917. To. 31st. July, 1917 (Volume 17.)		
War Diary	International Corner	01/07/1917	18/07/1917
War Diary	Proven	19/07/1917	31/07/1917
Heading	War Diary of the 29th Divisional Train. Army Service Corps. From 1st August 1917 to 31st August 1917. Volume 18		
War Diary	Proven	01/08/1917	07/08/1917
War Diary	Sheet 20 S/27.C.3.5	08/08/1917	29/08/1917
War Diary	Sheet 27 E/12.d.6.6	30/08/1917	31/08/1917

Heading	29th Divisional Train. War Diary. September 1917 In The Field 2-10-17, Vol 19		
War Diary	Proven	01/09/1917	19/09/1917
War Diary	20 S/27.C.3-5	20/09/1917	30/09/1917
Heading	29th. Divisional Train. War Diary for October, 1917. Volume 21		
War Diary	International Corner	01/10/1917	10/10/1917
War Diary	Proven.	11/10/1917	16/10/1917
War Diary	Basseux	17/10/1917	17/10/1917
War Diary	Hendecourt.	18/10/1917	31/10/1917
Heading	29th. Divisional Train. War Diary. Volumn 22. November 1917. Vol 21		
War Diary	Blaireville.	01/11/1917	05/11/1917
War Diary	Berles.	06/11/1917	18/11/1917
War Diary	Nurlu.	19/11/1917	30/11/1917
War Diary	Nurlu. (Fins Area)	01/12/1917	06/12/1917
War Diary	Manin.	07/12/1917	18/12/1917
War Diary	Hesdin	19/12/1917	31/12/1917
Heading	29th. Divisional Train. War Diary for the month of January, 1918. Vol 23		
War Diary	Hesdin	01/01/1918	03/01/1918
War Diary	Wizernes	05/01/1918	31/01/1918
War Diary	Poperinghe.	01/02/1918	11/02/1918
War Diary	Steenvoorde	12/02/1918	28/02/1918
Heading	War Diary 29 Div. Train 1-31 March 1918 Vol 25		
War Diary	Steenvoorde	01/03/1918	06/03/1918
War Diary	Poperinghe	07/03/1918	31/03/1918
Heading	29th. Divisional Train. War Diary for April, 1918 Vol 26		
War Diary	Brandhoek	01/04/1918	30/04/1918
Heading	29th. Divisional Train. War Diary for the month of May, 1918 Vol 27		
War Diary	Wallon Cappel.	01/05/1918	31/05/1918
Heading	29th. Divisional Train. War Diary, for the month of June, 1918.		
War Diary	Wallon Cappel.	01/06/1918	22/06/1918
War Diary	Wardrecques	23/06/1918	30/06/1918
Heading	29th. Divisional Train. War Diary for July, 1918. Vol 29		
War Diary	Wardrecques	01/07/1918	31/07/1918
War Diary	Bavinchove	01/08/1918	31/08/1918
War Diary	Borre.	01/09/1918	30/09/1918
War Diary	Brake Camp	01/10/1918	07/10/1918
War Diary	Vlamertinghe.	08/10/1918	13/10/1918
War Diary	Ypres.	14/10/1918	15/10/1918
War Diary	8/K. 7.c.8.9	16/10/1918	16/10/1918
War Diary	Ledgehem.	17/10/1918	20/10/1918
War Diary	Gulleghem.	21/10/1918	21/10/1918
War Diary	Courtrai.	22/10/1918	27/10/1918
War Diary	Mouveaux	28/10/1918	06/11/1918
War Diary	Rolleghem.	07/11/1918	13/11/1918
War Diary	Renaix.	14/11/1918	14/11/1918
War Diary	Flobecq.	15/11/1918	17/11/1918
War Diary	Enchein.	18/11/1918	20/11/1918
War Diary	Tubize.	21/11/1918	30/11/1918
War Diary		01/12/1918	31/12/1918

Heading	Rhine Army Southern Division Late 29th Division Divisional Train R.A.S.C. Jan-Oct 1919		
War Diary	Odenthal, Germany.	01/01/1919	28/02/1919
Heading	War Diary of Southern (late 29th) Divisional Train From 1/3/19 to 31/3/19 Volume 1		
War Diary	Odenthal	01/03/1919	31/03/1919
Heading	War Diary of Southern (late 29th) Divisional Train. From 1/4/19 to 30/4/19 Volume II		
War Diary	Odenthal	01/04/1919	17/09/1919
War Diary	Odenthal Germany.	18/09/1919	31/10/1919

Morrisberry 4/20/14

29TH DIVISION
DIVL TROOPS

29TH. DIVL TRAIN A.S.C.

MAR 1916 — ~~MAR 1918~~

Oct 1919

(225 — 228 Coy ASC)

To INDEPENDENT DIV

1/France/3.

W 74—664 250,000 3/15 L. S. & Co.

Army Form W. 3091.

Cover for Documents.

Nature of Enclosures.

Historical Account
of
29th Divisional Train
(225 & 228 Companies, A.S.C.)

Notes, or Letters written.

SECRET.

HISTORICAL ACCOUNT OF THE 29TH DIVISIONAL TRAIN.

JANUARY 11th 1915.	Divisional Train formed as the 40th Divisional Train at Aldershot.
FEBRUARY 11th 1915.	Unit moved to Buxton.
MAY 1st 1915.	Unit moved to Derby under the command of Major Molony.
MAY 14th 1915.	Unit was re-numbered as the 33rd Divisional Train.
JULY 26th 1915.	Unit moved to Clipstone.
AUGUST 28th 1915.	Unit moved to Bulford with the 33rd Division and went through intensive training with the Division.
NOVEMBER 12th 1915.	33rd Division proceeded overseas, taking with them the Supply Details and all the Transport Captains and Adjutant. During this period Major Molony handed over command of the Divisional Train to Major D.C.E.Grose.
NOVEMBER 17th 1915.	Major H.E.Sykes took over command of the Divisional Train from Major D.C.E.Grose.
NOVEMBER 19th 1915.	The Divisional Train was transferred as the 52nd Divisional Train and steps were then taken to convert it from Horse Transport to Mule Transport. Mules and Recruits arriving all through December and January.
JANUARY 28th 1916.	A.D.S.& T. Southern Command, inspected the Train which was now undergoing training. Companies were sent out 3 times a week to various farms to make camps, cook their dinners and returned in the evening.
FEBRUARY 5th 1916.	3 Brigade Companies left Bulford for Chisledon and the Headquarter Company remained at Bulford.
FEBRUARY 23rd 1916.	Information was received that we were re-numbered as the 29th Divisional Train and should proceed to France at an early date.
MARCH 7th 1916.	Official information arrived for re-numbering the Divisional Train as the 29th Divisional Train.
MARCH 9th 1916.	The Divisional Train went through a course of musketry during the ensuing week.
MARCH 20th 1916.	The Divisional Train left by 12 trains from Bulford and Chisledon respectively for Southampton and sailed the same evening on the "INVENTOR" and "BELLEROPHON".
MARCH 21st 1916.	Arrived at Havre and remained at the Rest Camp 2 days, proceeding by train at 8am on the 23rd March for Ailly le Clocher to join the 29th Division. Supply Officers and Supply Sections joined the Train from the Division.
MARCH 30th 1916.	The Divisional Train with the Division proceeded up country by march route.

APRIL 4th 1916.	Division went into the trenches.
MAY 9th 1916.	Mules were transferred for horses. Surplus personnel and Mules being evacuated to Abbeville Horse Transport Depot.
MAY 19th 1916.	Divisional Train was inspected by the G.O.C.Division.
MAY 24th 1916.	Divisional Train quartered in Arqueves and proceeded to make stables and standings.
JUNE 1st 1916.	Transport began to grow very heavy during this month owing to the enormous amount of stores being sent up in anticipation of the "Push". Animals feeling the strain and began to go down hill rapidly.
JUNE 24th 1916.	Bombardment preparatory to the "Push" started and during this period for the ensuing week the Divisional Train delivered rations up to the reserve trenches.
JULY 1st 1916.	General advance commenced and all night Baggage wagons of the Divisional Train were employed in bringing in wounded.
JULY 24th 1916.	The Division moved to back area preparatory to entraining for Flanders.
JULY 27th/28th.	Division entraining.
JULY 29th 1916.	Division arrived in the neighbourhood of Poperinghe.
AUGUST 8th 1916.	Gas Attack in the Ypres Salient. Driver Mewton awarded the Military Medal for conspicuous courage.
SEPTEMBER 11th 1916.	29th Divisional Artillery rejoined the Division from the Somme area, together with Headquarter Company.
	During the months of August and September the Divisional Train made standings and generally improved Camps, besides a great deal of fatigue work for the Division. The animals during this period picked up considerably.
OCTOBER 4th 1916.	Corps Commander, Lieut-General Sir Hunter Weston inspected the Divisional Train.
OCTOBER 6th 1916.	The Division moved to the Somme area.
OCTOBER 8th 1916.	The Division detrained in the neighbourhood of Amiens.
OCTOBER 18th 1916.	The Division finished moving into the Somme area, the Divisional Train being quartered at Albert.
DECEMBER 13th 1916.	The Division moved into the Rest Area, having been on the Somme front since their arrival in that Area. Animals very much pulled down by the hard work, and 20 pairs left behind for fatigue work.
JANUARY 10th 1917.	The Division moved back into the Somme Area. Horses and men having benefited very considerably from the rest, but owing to the bad state of the roads, were compelled to draw from Railhead in lieu of Motor Transport.
MARCH 3rd 1917.	The Division moved into the back area preparatory to moving elsewhere.

HONOURS & AWARDS.

OCTOBER 5th 1916.	T4/158090 Driver Mewton R.O.	Military Medal.
OCTOBER 28th 1916.	S4/056862 Private Kendall W.	Serbian Silver Medal, 2nd Class.
NOVEMBER 9th 1916.	S4/056806 S/Sgt.Cooper J.R.	Military Medal.
NOVEMBER 9th 1916.	S4/ 1053 Cpl. Whitbourn G.W.	Military Medal.
NOVEMBER 9th 1916.	S4/056769 Pte. Oatin A.G.	Military Medal.
JANUARY 1st 1917.	T/Lieut.Nightingale C.R.	Military Cross.
JANUARY 1st 1917.	Lieut-Col.Sykes H.E.	"Mentioned"
JANUARY 1st 1917.	Capt.Conran W.A.B.	"Mentioned"
JANUARY 1st 1917.	Lieut.Macmanaway R.T.R.	"Mentioned"
JANUARY 1st 1917.	T/20403 S.S.M.Ashton J.	"Mentioned"

XXXXXXXXX
XXXXXXXXX

Army Form C. 2118.

WAR DIARY
or
INTELLIGENCE SUMMARY

(Erase heading not required.)

1916

Place	Date	Hour	Summary of Events and Information	Remarks and references to Appendices
Left England.	March 20th.			
Havre.	Mar.21st.		Arrived Havre and went to Rest Camp.	
"	22nd.		Remainder at Rest Camp. Inspected by Camp Commandant. Disembarked all day. Reported to Camp Commandant. Reported Base Details and asked for orders. Told they knew nothing as we had no Base and to take them up country. Tried to see D. of T. but Base three times.	
"	23rd.		Left Havre with 226 Coy. followed by 227 Company.	
Ailly.	24th.		One man of 227 Company injured and left at Pont Remy Station. Arrived Ailly, arranged billets, snowing. Saw D.H.Q. and arranged to go to new area tomorrow.	
"	25th.		Met D.A.A.& Q.M.G. and went to new area by motor and visited C.H.A. Saw General Longmore. Last trains arrived. Went round billets.	
"	26th.		Saw D.A.A.& Q.M.G. and D.A.Q.M.G. about move also D.D.T. re motors. Base details returned to Havre.	
"	27th.		Inspected billets. Drew Mule for 225 for 147 Bde. R.F.A.	
"	28th.		Took over supplies and transport. Arrangements satisfactory. Conference at 2.pm. Everything altered and groups rearranged. Saw D.H.Q. R.A. 88th H.Q. R.A. 88th Bde.H.Q. 87th Bde.H.Q. D.H.Q.R.E. Refilling at 4.pm. for 88th Bde.Group.	
"	29th.		Refilling at 4.pm. for 87th Bde. Group.	
"	30th.		87th Bde. Group leaves for new area. 86th and H.Q.Group refill at 4.pm. 88th Bde.Group ordered to move up into 87th Bde.Group area. Capt.Siney reported 10.pm. all arranged.	
"	31st.		86th Bde. and H.Q. Group R.A. leave for new area. Adjt. and self an H.Q.party left for Beauquesne. New refillingpoint at Le Bon Air for 87th. 88th Bde.Group refill at 4.pm. 86th Bde.Group marched	

Army Form C. 2118.

WAR DIARY
or
INTELLIGENCE SUMMARY
(Erase heading not required.)

Instructions regarding War Diaries and Intelligence Summaries are contained in F.S. Regs., Part II. and the Staff Manual respectively. Title Pages will be prepared in manuscript.

Place	Date	Hour	Summary of Events and Information	Remarks and references to Appendices
Left England. March 20th.				
Havre.	Mar.21st.		Arrived Havre and went to Rest Camp. Disembarked all day. Reported to Camp Commandant.	
"	" 22nd.		Remainder at Rest Camp. Inspected by Camp Commandant. Reported Base Details and asked for Orders. Told they knew nothing as we had no Base and to take them up country. Tried to see D. of T. but Base three times.	
"	" 23rd.		Left Havre with 226 Coy. followed by 227 Company.	
Ailly.	" 24th.		One man of 227 Company injured and left at Pont Remy Station. Arrived Ailly, arranged billets, snowing. Saw D.H.Q. and arranged to go to new area tomorrow.	
"	" 25th.		Met D.A.A.& Q.M.G. and went to new area by motor and visited C.H.Q. Saw General Longmore. Last trains arrived. Went round billets.	
"	" 26th.		Saw D.A.A.& Q.M.G. and D.A.Q.M.G. about move also D.D.T. re motors. Base details returned to Havre.	
"	" 27th.		Inspected billets. Drew Mule for 225 for 147 Bde. R.F.A.	
"	" 28th.		Took over supplies and transport. Arrangements satisfactory. Conference at 2.pm. Everything altered and groups rearranged. Saw D.H.Q. R.A. 88th H.Q. 87th Bde.H.Q. D.H.Q.R.E. Refilling at 4.pm. for 88th Bde. Group.	
"	" 29th.		Refilling at 4.pm. for 87th Bde. Group.	
"	" 30th.		87th Bde. Group leaves for new area. 86th and H.Q.Group refill at 4.pm. 88th Bde.Group ordered to move up into 87th Bde.Group area. Capt.Simey reported 10.pm. all arranged.	
"	" 31st.		86th Bde. and H.Q.Group R.A. leave for new area. Adjt. and self and H.Q.party left for Beauquesne. New refillingpoint at Le Bon Air for 87th. 88th Bde.Group refil at 4.pm.	

Army Form C. 2118.

WAR DIARY
or
INTELLIGENCE SUMMARY
(Erase heading not required.)

Instructions regarding War Diaries and Intelligence Summaries are contained in F. S. Regs., Part II. and the Staff Manual respectively. Title Pages will be prepared in manuscript.

Place	Date	Hour	Summary of Events and Information	Remarks and references to Appendices
Le Havre	March 21	2.a.m.	Arrived at Le Havre by S.S. Ballarophon from Southampton. Disembarked at 7.a.m. and	
Sanvic	22		marched to rest camp at Sanvic. Total strengths 116 all ranks, 10 G.S. mules, 14 horses, 23 G.S. wagons, 2 kitchens, 1 water cart.	
	23		In camp at Sanvic.	
	24		Left camp 4.a.m. and entrained at Point 2. Le Havre. Proceeded to Point 6. Rouen, detrained and marched to Ailly le Haut Clocher arriving 1.15. a.m.	
Ailly le Haut Clocher	25		March. Animals on lines in field S. of village. Men in billets. Billets bad.	
Fameschon			Moved into new billets at Fameschon 12.p.m.	
	Sunday 26		Sent back 15 men of the base detachments under 1st Summonds to Le Havre 12.30.p.m. Visited Brigadier General of 85th Brigade. Took over 6 wagons, 12 men & 24 mules from No.1. C. Found wagons not fitted with brake bar strengthenings, mules not well shod and one mule with cuts	

2449 Wt. W14957/M99 750,000 1/16 J.B.C. & A. Forms/C.2118/12.

Army Form C. 2118.

WAR DIARY
or
INTELLIGENCE SUMMARY
(Erase heading not required.)

Instructions regarding War Diaries and Intelligence Summaries are contained in F. S. Regs., Part II. and the Staff Manual respectively. Title Pages will be prepared in manuscript.

Place	Date	Hour	Summary of Events and Information	Remarks and references to Appendices
Famechon	March 26		on rear hind boat, but extending into Fres.	
	27		Strength 113 of all ranks, 132 mules, 14 horses, 29 G.S. wagons, 2 limbers, 1 watercart.	
	28		At Famechon. Sent two Subalterns and 5 N.C.O.s to reconnoitre on roads & farms. 14 Supply details joined, also 25 loaders from Brigade units. Strength 152 of all ranks, and 2 officers Supply Section, total 154. Sent out 22 vehicles to Supply the various Brigade units. Refilling point on Abbeville – Amiens Rd. ¾ mile S. of Ailly. Went to Poix with S.S.M. Ashton to arrange billets.	
	29		Visited Brigadier at Bois de L'Abbaye. Sent out 13 wagons & 1 limber to supply units and sent 11 baggage wagons to units. Sent out 14 + 2 vehicles to supply units.	
	30		Visited Brigadier.	

2449 Wt. W14957/M90 750,000 1/16 J.B.C. & A. Forms/C.2118/12.

Army Form C. 2118.

WAR DIARY
or
INTELLIGENCE SUMMARY
(Erase heading not required.)

Instructions regarding War Diaries and Intelligence Summaries are contained in F. S. Regs., Part II. and the Staff Manual respectively. Title Pages will be prepared in manuscript.

Place	Date	Hour	Summary of Events and Information	Remarks and references to Appendices
Farrachon	March 31		Sent out 22 wagons to supply units. Refilled again at 4 p.m. and parked loaded wagons.	

29

Confidential

War Diary

No 4 Coy 29th Bn. Inf. Train A.S.C.

from April 1st - 1916 to April 30th 1916

Volume 2

Army Form C. 2118.

WAR DIARY
or
INTELLIGENCE SUMMARY

(Erase heading not required.)

Instructions regarding War Diaries and Intelligence Summaries are contained in F. S. Regs., Part II. and the Staff Manual respectively. Title Pages will be prepared in manuscript.

Place	Date	Hour	Summary of Events and Information	Remarks and references to Appendices
Beauquesne.	Apl.1st.		86th Brigade Group leave for new Area. Refilling Point for 87th and 86th Brigades at Le Bon Air. Refilling Point for Headquarter Group at Gorges. Saw C.O.C. re 1st line Transport which is very bad. Reported 88th Field Ambulance to A.D.M.S. re men riding on wagons and filling them with kits.	
"	2nd.		86th, 87th and 88th Brigades refil at Le Bon Air. 87th Brigade Group, less Iniskillings march to new area. 88th Brigad and Headquarter Group R.I. refil at Gorges.	
"	3rd.		86th Group refil Le Bon Air. H.Q.Div.Units attached. 87th " " Acheux & Leavillers Road. 88th " " Gorges H.Q. Group R.A. refil " 87	
Raincheval.	4th.		88th Brigade went into trenches. 86th Brigade and 88th Brigade moved up into area. Refilling at Acheux Leavillers for R.I. at Gorges.	
"	5th.		½ 15th and 17th Brigades R.A. and ½ 132nd Brigade/R.A. moved to positions.	
"	6th.		The other ½ of 15th and 17th Brigades and ½ 132nd Brigade moved up to positions. New refilling point at Raincheval.	
"	7th.		Ordered to return Car. All Cars under S.S.O. Heavy firing.	
"	8th.		Last day at Raincheval refilling point. Changed Mule lines as owner complained of eating trees old damage. Pte.Cardus and Car No.235 returned to Abbeville.	
"	9th.		Refilled at Railhead (Belle Eglise) H.Q.Coy. moved to Amplier. S.S.O and Adjt. went with A.Q.M.G. re Reserve Trenches.	
"	10th.		Went to D.H.Q. re move. Saw Bdr.88th Brigade at Louvencourt. Saw G.O.C. re Div. mark. Returned via Amplier and Le Bon Air, saw refilling. Took wagon at 5 p.m. with new mark for Division.C.O.C. satisfied and sanctioned it officially. Returned via Vauchelles, saw O.C. 31st D.T. exchanged views. S.S.O. left for leave and Capt.Bell took his place and everything	

2449 Wt. W14957/M90 750,000 1/16 J.B.C. & A. Forms/C.2118/12.

Army Form C. 2118.

WAR DIARY
or
INTELLIGENCE SUMMARY
(Erase heading not required.)

Instructions regarding War Diaries and Intelligence Summaries are contained in F.S. Regs., Part II. and the Staff Manual respectively. Title Pages will be prepared in manuscript.

Place	Date	Hour	Summary of Events and Information	Remarks and references to Appendices
Raincheval.	Apl.10th (Continued)		Working like clockwork. Saw all C.O's and S.O's of Companies and gave them General instructions. Another Motor to be withdrawn, intricate for P.O's to do the work without. Started making troughs. Lovely day warm, but roads very dusty.	
"	11th.		Heavy day with Transport. Rained and made roads difficult for both animals and motors. Arranged billets for Train at Louvencourt. Water scarce, saw R.E. about pumps who suggested digging troughs from Raincheval. Went to Amplier, difficulties with refilling without Transport. 2 mules reported died on 10th. Arranged move round of battalions moving up. 2nd blanket to be withdrawn also goat skin jerkins.	
"	12th.		Billeting arrangements at Louvencourt by 4 Coy. representatives. Very cramped for room, water arrangements bad. Move of 87th Brigade to locations of 86th Bde. to 87th and 88th Bde. to 86th to be finally completed on 13th. Bdes. do not appear to grasp what baggage wagons are for. Dearth of cold shoers in Infantry. 1st Line transport suggested training some. Mule shoes still very slow in coming in. Rained all day, mud very bad for motor traction.	
"	13th.		Visited D.H.Q. with reference to parking wagons of the Train at Louvencourt, visited that place with D.A.A. & Q.M.G. satisfactorily arranged. Remainder of Infantry Brigades moved over. Difficulty found in purchasing Straw. All leave cancelled. Pte.P at and Vauxhall Car returned to 4th Army Troops Supply Column. Rained incessantly.	
Louvencourt.	14th.		Train concentrated at Louvencourt. Very cramped for room in billets. Straw still very difficult owing to lack of Motor Cars. Cars required on account of distance. S.S.O. recalled off leave. Billets left very dirty by 86th Brigade. Fine day but cold.	
"	15th.		Refilling much better. Railway late in loading. Improving billets and clearing up the last units very dirty. Hostile Aeroplane passed over dropping red and white lights over Belle Eglise reported it to D.iv.Hd.Qrs.	

(2)

2449 Wt. W14957/Mgo 750,000 1/16 J.B.C. & A. Forms/C.2118/12.

Army Form C. 2118.

WAR DIARY
or
INTELLIGENCE SUMMARY
(Erase heading not required.)

Instructions regarding War Diaries and Intelligence Summaries are contained in F. S. Regs., Part II. and the Staff Manual respectively. Title Pages will be prepared in manuscript.

Place	Date	Hour	Summary of Events and Information	Remarks and references to Appendices
Louvencourt.	Apl.16th.		Refilling improving. Water arrangements bad. Started S.T.O. at Railhead and Refilling Points. D.A.Q.M.G. and D.A.A. & Q.M.G. visited camp.	
"	17th.		369th Battery lent to 48th Division. 5 Mules sent to Mobile Veterinary Section. Received advance pay books for Officers. Much correspondence in. Very heavy rain with squalls.	
"	18th.		More Artillery moving up. 86th and 88th Brigades both began to take up line. S.S.O. returned from leave. Car W.239 damaged. Summary of evidence in case of Dr. Patterson taken. Hospital Comforts coming up, badly. No.89th Field Ambulance supplied. Raining heavily. 369th Battery wagons not returned. mules lines getting very bad.	
"	19th.		Very heavy rain and billets and mule lines in a very bad state. R.E. will not sanction use of Quarries.	
"	20th.		Capt.Bell reported to D.A.Q.M.S. for instruction in Staff duties. Inspected billets, not enough attention paid to keeping straw dry. Empty tins left lying about. Mules lines could be improved with more care. No. 4 and No. 1 Companies expecially bad, not enough energy shewn in these two Companies. Arranged to fetch ashes from Doullens on Friday. Lieut.Lachard in charge. Very heavy rain but looks clearer at night. Arranged with O.C. Turcelling Company to fetch rations earlier.	
"	21st.		Lieut. Lachard fetched 15 cubic yards of Cinders from Doullens which have proved of great value in making pathways. Units still at fault not indenting in time for special supplies and expecting them to be supplied at once. Field Ambulances especially at fault. Fine morning but turned into heavy rain, lines very bad. Supply refilling much improved.	

Army Form C. 2118.

WAR DIARY
or
INTELLIGENCE SUMMARY

(Erase heading not required.)

Instructions regarding War Diaries and Intelligence Summaries are contained in F. S. Regs., Part II. and the Staff Manual respectively. Title Pages will be prepared in manuscript.

Place	Date	Hour	Summary of Events and Information	Remarks and references to Appendices
Louvencourt.	April 22nd.		Went to Doullens to purchase paint and arrange for more ashes. Raining very heavily.	
"	23rd.		Supply Railway Train very late (7hrs.) owing to breakdown. Heard Royal Scots were leaving the Division. No arrangements made until 8.30.pm. Beautiful fine day, country drying.	
"	24th.		Royal Scots left the Command. Capt.Vivcash took 4 lorries for Cinders to Doullens. 16th Middlesex arrived from Doullens for 86th Brigade. D.A.Q.M.G. handed over to Capt.Bell whilst on leave. Went to Mailly and saw O.C.86th Infantry Brigade. Great Aerial activity. Fine day, dull towards evening.	
"	25th.		Royal Munster Fusiliers leave for Boulogne. Had to supply Blanket Wagons which are not supplied by war establishment, Part VII for Divisional Train equipped for Egypt. Heavy firing during the night. Great improvement made in Lines. Water Supply causing great grave difficulties. Beautiful day with cool breeze. Aerial activity.	
"	26th.		Went to Acheux. Saw C.F.W. re water at Louvencourt. Leaving roads in H.Q.Billet. Improving standings. Fixed the temporary refilling point round Louvencourt. Beautiful day, very hot. All the main streets named, find great use to ORDERLIES.	
"	27th.		Move over of Brigades. Infy. 86th and 87th. Drawing Cinders, two journeys. Completion of local purchase of paint for wagon covers. Bomb dump blown up at Forceville. Went to suggested refilling point between Forceville and Bertrancourt fairly satisfactory in fine weather. First day capstan pump in use, very satisfactory. Heavy firing to the north and south of us. Beautiful day, very hot and getting very dusty.	
"	28th.		A.Q.M.G. 29th Division inspected Divisional Train Camp. Went to Doullens to purchase twine. C.Q.M.S. Tucker reported from Base. Orders re rucksacks.Obtained 5000 from R.F. at Englebelmer. Saddlers all mobilized for the work in Billet No.160 under S.Sgt.Saddler No. 3 Coy. Move of 86th and 87th Infy. Bdes. satisfactorily arranged. Heavy firing during the night on our flanks. Beautiful day.	

Army Form C. 2118.

WAR DIARY
or
INTELLIGENCE SUMMARY

(Erase heading not required.)

Instructions regarding War Diaries and Intelligence Summaries are contained in F. S. Regs., Part II. and the Staff Manual respectively. Title Pages will be prepared in manuscript.

Place	Date	Hour	Summary of Events and Information	Remarks and references to Appendices
Louvencourt.	April 29th.		Arrangements made for transport of reserve rations and water for Forts. Heard Mules were to be changed for Horses H.Q. regret necessity of change. Went to D.H.Q. as usual. Found a gun limber broken. Heavy firing at 11pm. raid taking place. Mule died of twisted gut. Beautiful day.	
"	30th.		Final arrangements made for reserve. Arranged washing of Petrol Tins for Reserve. Went to Bxx. R.A.H.Q. and D.H.Q. Thunder shower. Nothing important happened during the day.	

2449 Wt. W14957/M90 750,000 1/16 J.B.C. & A. Forms/C.2118/12.

Army Form C. 2118.

WAR DIARY
or
INTELLIGENCE SUMMARY
(Erase heading not required.)

Instructions regarding War Diaries and Intelligence Summaries are contained in F. S. Regs., Part II. and the Staff Manual respectively. Title Pages will be prepared in manuscript.

Place	Date	Hour	Summary of Events and Information	Remarks and references to Appendices
Franchon	April 1		Moved to Fieffes 8 a.m. to 2 p.m. - into fair billets, all animals in stables. Supply wagons delivering supplies in route to units. A good supply of water & straw for watering animals & washing wagons	
	Sunday 2		Sent out 13 wagons & 1 limber to supply units. Refilling point at point 151.	
	3		" "	
	4		Refilled at 10 a.m. and moved with full wagons to Raincheval supplying units en route. Machine Gun Co. Transferred to 31st Division from this date.	
Raincheval	5		Refilling point at Louvilliers on Louvilliers - Acheux Rd. Supplied units & 12 wagons & 1 limber. Visited Brigadier at Louvencourt	
	6		Visited Brigadier at Louvencourt. Refilling point 10 a.m. on Raincheval - Vauchelles rd. Sent out 12 wagons and 1 limber to units. Proceeded to Acheux	

2449 Wt. W14957/M90 750,000 1/16 J.B.C. & A. Forms/C.2118/12.

WAR DIARY
or
INTELLIGENCE SUMMARY

(Erase heading not required.)

Army Form C. 2118.

Instructions regarding War Diaries and Intelligence Summaries are contained in F. S. Regs., Part II. and the Staff Manual respectively. Title Pages will be prepared in manuscript.

Place	Date	Hour	Summary of Events and Information	Remarks and references to Appendices
Ruitz	April			
	7		at 5 p.m. to Gadonne Stones. 11 baggage wagons returned from units to park at Ruitzwald.	
	8		R.E. calling Co. ordered to strength. Sent out 13 wagons and 1 limber. Also 1 wagon baggage section to Louvencourt. Visited Brigadier at Louvencourt.	
			Sent out 13 wagons + 1 limber to units, 2nd Lt. Pirrie in charge. Also 1 wagon from baggage section to Louvencourt. Visited Brigadier at Louvencourt. To returned at Curlus with Capt. Francks, S.O.	
	Friday 9		Sent out 13 wagons + 1 limber to supply units. Visited first line transport at Louvencourt, Essex, Hants, and effected changes fittings in harness.	

WAR DIARY or INTELLIGENCE SUMMARY

Army Form C. 2118.

(Erase heading not required.)

Instructions regarding War Diaries and Intelligence Summaries are contained in F. S. Regs., Part II. and the Staff Manual respectively. Title Pages will be prepared in manuscript.

Place	Date	Hour	Summary of Events and Information	Remarks and references to Appendices
Lavacourt Ravenshead	April 10		Visited and inspected the first line transport of the Royal Scots at Acquires and the Reinforcements at Lavacourts. Sent out wand transport.	
	11		To Lavacourts and arranged billets for men there. Sent out wand transports to visit.	
	12		Sent out wand transport. Visited Brigadier.	
	13		To Lavacourt, arranged transport, to Acheux and Sarton to Corps Cashier.	
	14		Moved from Ravenshead into new billets at Lavacourt. Billets fair, water supply bad, only available water drawn by hand from wells. Horse lines	
Lavacourt			in field outside village on Vauchelles Rd.	
	15		Visited Brigadier at his H.Qrs at Englebelmer.	
	16		To Brigade H.Qrs.	
	17		To Railhead at Belle Eglise 7.a.m. in charge of Traffic. At present the Div. Train	

Army Form C. 2118.

WAR DIARY
or
INTELLIGENCE SUMMARY
(Erase heading not required.)

Instructions regarding War Diaries and Intelligence Summaries are contained in F. S. Regs., Part II and the Staff Manual respectively. Title Pages will be prepared in manuscript.

Place	Date	Hour	Summary of Events and Information	Remarks and references to Appendices
Louvencourt	April 17		have to discharge the trains at railhead. Carry supplies to refilling points, gets again and proceed to units. Railway staff arrived late. Evacuated 2 mules to Mons Vet Sec.	
	18		To Brigade Hd. Qrs and also went round first line transports at Acheux.	
	19		To Doullens and bought horse clippers for Co.	
	20		To Brigade Hd.qrs.	
	21		To Brigade Hd.qrs. Paid the Co. in afternoon.	
	22		To railhead in charge of traffic. Found all correct and checked the Div. Train by 6.50 a.m. To Brigade at 3.30 p.m.	
	23		Royal Scots left the Brigade - Scots train baggage wagons to Beaumont at 9 a.m. and then supplies districts to Doullens. Went to Amplier and arranged billets there	
	24		for the night for 20 mules, 10 men & one officer.	

WAR DIARY or INTELLIGENCE SUMMARY

Army Form C. 2118.

Place	Date	Hour	Summary of Events and Information	Remarks and references to Appendices
Louvencourt	April 25		Returned 2 baggage and 2 supply wagons to 225 Co. to Royal Scots having left the Brigade. Strength 147 all ranks 106 mules 31 vehicles	
	26		On duty at railhead 7.a.m. to 10.a.m. Visited Beaumont at 11.20. a.m. To Beauquesne at 2.30. to see Supply Coe. Workshop Officer re repairs to horse in Louvencourt.	
	27		Supply Section on duty, 15 wagons + 1 limber.	
	28		Baggage Section on duty, no change in units.	
	29		Visited Brigade Hd Qrs at 5.a.m. Sents out usual Transport. Supply section on duty at 5. p.m.	
	30		To Brigade Hd Qrs 11 a.m. Sents out usual Transport. Baggage Section on duty	

Army Form C. 2118.

WAR DIARY
or
INTELLIGENCE SUMMARY

(Erase heading not required.)

Instructions regarding War Diaries and Intelligence Summaries are contained in F. S. Regs., Part II. and the Staff Manual respectively. Title Pages will be prepared in manuscript.

Place	Date	Hour	Summary of Events and Information	Remarks and references to Appendices
LOUVENCOURT	May 1st 1916.		Had all the water cans for Forts washed and filled. Sent Capt. Upson for more twine to DOULLENS. Visited D.F.O. morning and evening. Reserve rations for Forts came in. Beautiful day, shower in evening. Heavy firing during the night.	
"	2nd.		Visited D.H.Q. in morning. Went to Headquarters 36th Divisional Train to judge wagon competition. 36th Divisional Train arrived at a pitch of excellence as regards harness and clean agonsand General turnout, difficult to conceive on active service. The reserve rations put into AUCHONVILLERS and the Forts satisfactorily. No firing. Cool day with breeze. Saw A.D. of S & T. 4th Army.	
"	3rd.		Two Vauxhall Cars broken, repaired same evening. Issued instructions re page of Cars. Visited D.H.Q. in evening.	
"	4th.		Went to D.H.C. in the morning with water carriers. Orders that ACH UX-LLAIVILLRS road closed after 4. pm. O.C. 36th Divisional Train called gave him some notes on supply arrangements.	
"	5th.		Wagons being washed and rubbed with wood preserving oil, great improvement. Went to Famechon to see O.C. 48th Divisional Train re coal at SONASTRE and other centres. Took S.S.O. Sent Adjutant to DOULLENS to make arrangements re green vegetables. He reports difficult to get. Very thundery.	
"	6th.		Lieutenants Sergeant and Hunt returned off leave. Arranged water carriers for AUCHONVILLERS. Visited D.H.Q. in the evening. Wet night.	
"	7th.		Quiet day. Cold and damp.	
"	8th.		Heard Horses were arriving. Rainy.	

(Continued)

Army Form C. 2118.

WAR DIARY
or
INTELLIGENCE SUMMARY

(Erase heading not required.)

Instructions regarding War Diaries and Intelligence Summaries are contained in F. S. Regs, Part II. and the Staff Manual respectively. Title Pages will be prepared in manuscript.

Place	Date	Hour	Summary of Events and Information	Remarks and references to Appendices
LOUVENCOURT.	May 9th.		Wagon Competition judged by Bdr.O.C.29th Division R.A. Went to AUXI-LE-CHATEAU and on to CANAPLES, met R.D.Horses and left guide. Horses arrived 3.50.pm. Water sent up to AUCHONVILLERS. Prepared 270 Mules and 32 men for ABBEVILLE. Visited H.Q.31st Divisional Train. Went to D.H.Q. Very wet.	
"	" 10th.		Mules and Men left for ABBEVILLE 7.30.am. In spite of orders to leave at 6.30.am. Conducting Officer did not seem to have any initiative.	
"	" 11th.		Went to CANAPLES to meet horses. Animals in poor condition. Went to D.H.Q. in evening. Very warm.	
"	" 12th.		EAST SURREY Y.COMPANY left Division with Train Transport. Horses arrived from ABBEVILLE. Visited new refilling point with S.S.O. and inspected new road to TOLLESBY TR. Saw G.O.C. who expressed a wish to inspect the Train at an early date. Sultry and inclined to thunder.	
"	" 13th.		270 Mules left for ABBEVILLE via AUXI-LE-CHATEAU under Lieut.Major.	
"	" 14th.		CYCLIST COMPANY left Division with Train Transport. Remainder of Mules and surplus personnel left for ABBEVILLE under Lieut.Smith. G.O.C. gave orders for draining Bde.Coy.Lines. Very wet.	
"	" 15th.		F.G.C.M. on Dr.Velvick. Started draining wagon park and general cleaning up. Rained in early morning. Improvement in the afternoon. Heavy firing at night. Fine evening with sun.	
"	" 16th.		Ordered roofing to be prepared 1. horse lines. Went to Div.S.C.about Cars and Motor Cycles. Tried heat on debilitated horses. More wagons for R.2.work. Wagons shewing signs of wear. Pump broke down. Great aerial activity. Beautiful fine day, hot sun.	
"	" 17th.		Drains in wagon par finished. Hd.Qr.Coy.improving sanitation. More efficient measures taken for burning manure. Visited R.A.line MAILLY. Fine day.	

(Continued)

Army Form C. 2118.

WAR DIARY
or
INTELLIGENCE SUMMARY

(Erase heading not required.)

Instructions regarding War Diaries and Intelligence Summaries are contained in F. S. Regs., Part II. and the Staff Manual respectively. Title Pages will be prepared in manuscript.

Place	Date	Hour	Summary of Events and Information	Remarks and references to Appendices
LOUVRECOURT.	May 18th.		Improvements in sanitation. Fine day.	
"	19th.		Inspection by G.O.C.Division. Satisfactory. Much aerial activity. Very satisfactory, results saves loss. dumping ried/alfalfa.	
"	20th.		Improved standing round pumps. Went to DOULLENS to purchase paint drugs etc. Made arrangements re green forage. Fine day and very hot.	
"	21st.		Went to ENGLEBELMER about Straw. A.Q.M.G. ordered move of Train to ACHEUX.	
"	22nd.		Went to ACHEUX and took notes of new accommodation. Informed A.Q.M.G. Heavy explosion near LOUVRECOURT. Oats for Train bad, some germinating. Water supply failing. Very hot and slight shower in the evening.	
"	23rd.		Water supply still failing. A.Q.M.G. informed me ACHEUX was not to be Train destination. Visited ARUUVES, very suitable for Divisional Train. Reported at 6.30.pm. to A.Q.M.G. who ordered Train to move there by 26th. Fourth Division moved through. Very hot, cool breeze at night.	
"	24th.		Visited ARQUVES for allotment of billets. Began to rain in evening, very wet at night.	
"	25th.		O.C. Companies visited ARQUVES. Visited R.H.Q. Very wet. Inspected 1st Line Transport, 87th Brigade.	
"	26th.		Monsieur Rossat left for leave. Went to DOULLENS. Visited D.H.Q. in evening. Inspected 1st Line Transport 87th Brigade.	
ARQUVES.	27th.		29th Divisional Train moved to ARQUVES. Inspected vacated billets and found them clean. Visited D.H.Q. in evening.	

Army Form C. 2118.

WAR DIARY
or
INTELLIGENCE SUMMARY
(Erase heading not required.)

Instructions regarding War Diaries and Intelligence Summaries are contained in F. S. Regs., Part II. and the Staff Manual respectively. Title Pages will be prepared in manuscript.

Place	Date	Hour	Summary of Events and Information	Remarks and references to Appendices
ARQUEVES.	May 28th.		Visited several places for material for horse lines.	
"	" 29th.		ACHEUX shelled. Started making horse lines. New allotment of leave received. One clerk sent to M.T.Depot, Havre. Very wet in the evening.	
"	" 30th.		Men making drainage trenches and horse lines and improving standings. 14 wagons went to AUCHONVILLERS for material, returned full. ACHEUX shelled. Fine day.	
"	" 31st.		4 Transport Officers of 86th Brigade joined for instruction. Horse lines continued. Lecture on Stable Management and horse standings. Visited by D.A.Q.M.G. and Claims Officer. Fine day, hot sun.	
	31.5.16.			

(Sgd) W.E.Sykes
Lieut-Col. ASC.
Commdg. 29th Divisional Train.

2449 Wt. W14957/M90 750,000 1/16 J.B.C. & A. Forms/C.2118/12.

Army Form C. 2118.

WAR DIARY
or
INTELLIGENCE SUMMARY
(Erase heading not required.)

Instructions regarding War Diaries and Intelligence Summaries are contained in F.S. Regs., Part II. and the Staff Manual respectively. Title Pages will be prepared in manuscript.

Place	Date	Hour	Summary of Events and Information	Remarks and references to Appendices
ARQUEVES.	June 1st.		Went to Refilling Point, not satisfied with the tidiness of Dumps. Bricks fetched from AUCHONVILLERS. Made good headway with lines. Visited D.H.Q. in the evening. ACHEUX STATION shelled in morning. Fine hot day.	
"	" 2nd.		Horse Lines still making headway. Class of Transport Officers finished. Visited D.H.Q. Dumps altered and remaining dumps of Acheux-Lealvillers road taken over from 38th Divl.Train. Fine day.	
"	" 3rd.		Detailed by Division to attend 4th Division Horse Show. Fine day with showers. Heard of Naval Action in North Sea.	
"	" 4th.		--	
"	" 5th.		Visited D.H.Q. in the morning. Col.Abbott asked for a report on the roads to the trenches. Wet and cold.	
"	" 6th.		Put into Reserve Trenches reserve rations. Party fired on about midnight, but probably only in expectation of relieving firing line. Visited firing lines and went round all the roads round AUCHONVILLERS, MAILLY-MAILLET, and ENGLEBELMER only fit in fine weather want much repairing. Colle very bad amongst the horses. Very wet.	
"	" 7th.		Reserve rations put into AUCHONVILLERS DUMP. All quiet and satisfactory. News of sinking of the Hampshire with Lord Kitchener received. Visited D.H.Q. and arranged to get bricks for Rotten Row. Arranged to go with Col.Abbott to view roads and make arrangements. Roads very full of Motor Transport at night.	
"	" 8th.		Ordered Lieut.King to fetch 12 loads of bricks from AUCHONVILLERS for repair of ACHEUX WOOD ROAD. Returned 6.30.following morning. Went with A.Q.M.G. round the roads between MAILLY and ACHEUX. Unmetalled roads impassable in wet weather. Heavy rain.	
"	" 9th.		Arranged permanent fatigue of 2 wagons from AUCHONVILLERS carting bricks, billeted at MAILLY. Went to D.H.Q. with Lieut.Hulme to explain American way of making brush roads. C.R.E. not very taken with the idea. Very wet.	

Army Form C. 2118.

WAR DIARY
or
INTELLIGENCE SUMMARY
(Erase heading not required.)

Instructions regarding War Diaries and Intelligence Summaries are contained in F.S. Regs., Part II and the Staff Manual respectively. Title Pages will be prepared in manuscript.

Place	Date	Hour	Summary of Events and Information	Remarks and references to Appendices
ARQUEVES.	June 10th.		Made arrangements for balance of Reserve rations to go up on Sunday. Arranged to have ARQUEVES-LEALVILLERS road re-opened for convoy. Very wet.	
"	" 11th.		Transport Officers of 88th Brigade reported for short class.	
"	" 12th.		Major Lawson went on leave. Went to D.H.Q. Arranged petrol tins for 87th Brigade and to be sent to AUCHONVILLERS. Very wet.	
"	" 13th.		Sent Petrol Tins to Louvencourt (1100) Petrol Tins sent to AUCHONVILLERS. Wet.	
"	" 14th.		Arranged to take rails on empty supply wagons from ENGLEBELMER to MAILLY. Very busy. More Petrol Tins sent up. Fine.	
"	" 15th.		17 Horses handed over to Lancashire Hussars. Went round ENGLEBELMER and MAILLY. Visited D.H.Q. Fine.	
"	" 16th.		Visited D.H.Q. 5 horses handed over to Lancashire Hussars. Visited Trenches to view the roads with O.C.Companies. Heavy firing. Major Lawson died on leave. Very fine.	
"	" 17th.		Visited trenches AUCHONVILLERS and with all Officers to view the roads for advance. Sent up more petrol tins to ENGLEBELMER. Many aeroplanes up. Very fine.	
"	" 18th.		Sent up N.C.O's with Transport Officers to view roads from trenches. Took O.C.No. 3 with me in afternoon and officer i/c fatigue party to mark forward roads. Much aerial activity. Heavy firing probably ranging. Visited Kent R.E.	
"	" 19th.		Lieut.King fetched bricks for new road at MAILLY WOOD. VISITED bridges over trenches with O.C.No. 3 Coy. Detailed Lieut.Pirouet and 10 men to make chalk line on right side of road as guide to wagons. Dull.	
"	" 20th.		Visited new Mailly wood road, saw R.E. 12 more loads of bricks required, detailed Lieut. King to fetch them. Water Carts sent to ENGLEBELMER as water supply broken down. Water carts kept. Visited 48th Divl.Train about wagons for R.A.being lent to 29th Division. Heavy firing. German aeroplane supposed to have landed near. Fine day.	

Army Form C. 2118.

WAR DIARY
or
INTELLIGENCE SUMMARY
(Erase heading not required.)

Place	Date	Hour	Summary of Events and Information	Remarks and references to Appendices
ARQUEVES.	June 21st.		Water Carts to be kept till tanks filled. Major Jackson reported. Went round Brigades and visited all roads to trenches etc. Heavy firing. Much aerial activity. Very fine and dry. Extra Water Carts sent to ENGLEBELMER.	
"	22nd.		Went round Brigades with Major Jackson also D.H.Q. Visited roads. Had orders to make bomb proofs for Train at MAILLY WOOD.	
"	23rd.		Visited MAILLY WOOD inspected progress of roads. Went with O.C.Hd.Qr.Coy. to view forward roads. O.C.Hd.Qr.Coy. and Captains selected sites for Camps in MAILLY WOOD. Intermittent shelling on both sides. Very heavy thunder storms and heavy rain during the night.	
"	24th.		Bombardment started. Made bomb proofs at MAILLY WOOD.	
"	25th.		Continued making dug outs and horse covers at MAILLY WOOD. Heavy firing. All waggons returned safely. Rxxxxxx. Dresden.	
"	26th.		Dresden 10.15. Party left for MAILLY WOOD under Major Jackson. Water Carts left for 86th Bde.	
"	27th.		1 Water Cart to R.A.H.Q. 5 Water Carts arrived from VIII Corps. Bombardment very heavy. Went to MAILLY WOOD in the evening. Two days rations put into trenches successfully. Very wet.	
"	28th.		Companies still preparing dug-outs and shelters at MAILLYWOOD. "Z" day postponed. Very wet.	
"	29th.		Roads very bad and repair gangs put on in ACHEUX WOOD. MAILLY WOOD parties still at work. Refilling at 10.am. and delivered to Units for 1st. Visited D.H.Q. with Major Jackson. Bombardment continues, more German firing than previously. Drier and no rain.	
"	30th.		Heavy rain all night, but drying wind towards morning. Refilling/owing to train being late late Move postponed till July 2nd. Visited D.H.Q. at 10.pm. Rotten Row open to all traffic. Dry wind and fine.	

F.W.M. Lieut-Col. ASC.
Commdg.29th Divl.Train.

CONFIDENTIAL.

WAR DIARY OF

29TH DIVISIONAL TRAIN A.S.C.

FROM JULY 1st 1916   TO   JULY 31st 1916.

(VOLUME 5.)

Army Form C. 2118.

WAR DIARY
or
INTELLIGENCE SUMMARY

(Erase heading not required.)

Instructions regarding War Diaries and Intelligence Summaries are contained in F. S. Regs., Part II. and the Staff Manual respectively. Title Pages will be prepared in manuscript.

Place	Date	Hour	Summary of Events and Information	Remarks and references to Appendices
ARQUEVES.	July 1st.		Advance begun. 29th Division held up at Pt.Q.17 a. Attack successful right and left. Feeding strength down 7,000. 48th Division pushed forward in support. 25 wagons turned out to pick up wounded. Fine day.	
"	2nd.		3 Battalions 88th Brigade attached to 48th Division. Still being fed by 29th Division. 88th Division being held in reserve. 48th Division went into trenches. Fine hot day. Wounded nearly all evacuated also 500 prisoners.	
"	3rd.		Wounded and stragglers still coming in. Went to Mailly. Visited D.H.Q. re proposed move, orders received to stand by. Wagons very late returning after delivering rations. One Driver wounded. Very wet in evening.	
"	4th.		Arranged Salvage of Brigade Dumps. 87th Brigade take over to rive Ancre. Move of 86th Brigade to reserve. Very wet and heavy shelling on both sides. Wagons with rations very late returning.	
"	5th.		Visited D.H.Q. and then 87th Brigade Headquarters, travelled by motor via Martinsart, left Car on Mesnil Road. Shelled in Mesnil. Went to Hamel. Inspected roads, impassable through Mesnil. Road excellent through Avelly Wood under cover. Found Car had been hit. Returned Arqueves found many moves arranged. Fine afternoon. Transferred to the Reserve Army.	
"	6th.		All wagons from night convoys returned without casualties. Sussex Regiment arrived. Convoys to Hamel and Knightsbridge fired on at night. Very wet.	
"	7th.		19th Northumberland Fusiliers (Pioneers) arrived and attached to Division. Detachment under Lieut.King stationed at MAILLY. Horses begining to show signs of hard wear and losing condition. 2 Horses wounded at Hamel. Very wet.	
"	8th.		Visited Detachment at MAILLY. Saw D.H.Q. reported animals as being too hard worked. One Driver wounded by shrapnel. Fine day.	
"	9th.		Startedhew detachment at ACHEUX. Visited detachment at Mailly. Very heavy firing. Lovely day.	

Army Form C. 2118.

WAR DIARY
or
INTELLIGENCE SUMMARY
(Erase heading not required.)

Instructions regarding War Diaries and Intelligence Summaries are contained in F. S. Regs., Part II. and the Staff Manual respectively. Title Pages will be prepared in manuscript.

Place	Date	Hour	Summary of Events and Information	Remarks and references to Appendices
ARQUEVES.	July 10th.		French reached outskirts of Peronne. Transport working more smoothly. Very fine day.	
"	11th.		Reserve Park took on fatigues. Horses allowed Linseed Cake. Went Amiens to try and obtain cake but found Doullens cheaper. Made water tanks out of sheets. Fine but cold.	
"	12th.		Went to D.H.Q. Dresden at night. Cold little rain. Australians passing through.	
"	13th.		Further advance. Started repairing dumps. Fine day but cold.	
"	14th.		Water Carts returning from Division. Convoy loading stored at Mesnil shelled. Cpl. of fatigue party killed. Troops advancing. Two cases of mange in No. 3 Coy. Fine day.	
"	15th.		Arranged Fresh Vegetables at Amiens. Corps Commander inspected the Train and expressed his satisfaction. News of further advance. Sussex Regiment left rationed to and for 16th. Fine day.	
"	16th.		Mange discovered, strict precautions being taken. Wet.	
"	17th.		Improving Horse Lines. Orvillers captured. Very wet. Bombardment during night. Dresden 10.pm.	
"	18th.		Three animals evacuated, 2 with mange. Visited Amiens re vegetables. Orders received for water carts to be sent to 46th Reserve Park. Heavy firing. Very wet but fine towards evening.	
"	19th.		Eastern portion of Deville Wood captured by enemy day previous also northern portion of Longueval village. Inspection of 88th Brigade by Major Jackson. A.A.& Q.M.G.visited Train. Train ordered by VIII Corps into camp. Visited new camping ground. Visited D.H.Q. in the evening. Beautiful day with fine drying sun.	
"	20th.		Orders to move following day. Cleared Arqueves. Visited D.H.Q.	
IN CAMP NEAR VAUCHELLES.	21st.		Marched into Vauchelles Camp, good camping ground. Beautiful day. A.A. & Q.M.G. visited Camp.	

2449 Wt. W14957/M90 750,000 1/16 J.B.C. & A. Forms/C.2118/12.

Army Form C. 2118.

WAR DIARY
or
INTELLIGENCE SUMMARY

(Erase heading not required.)

Instructions regarding War Diaries and Intelligence Summaries are contained in F. S. Regs., Part II. and the Staff Manual respectively. Title Pages will be prepared in manuscript.

Place	Date	Hour	Summary of Events and Information	Remarks and references to Appendices
IN CAMP NEAR VAUCHELLES.	July 22nd.		Arranged movements. Visited 25th Division to make arrangements re taking over. Fine day.	
"	23rd.		Arranging move. 88th Brigade moved to Beauval with No. 4 Company. 86th Brigade moved to Bus.	
"	24th.		86th Brigade moved to Beauval with No. 2 Company. 87th Brigade moved to Bus. Visited Companies. Visited D.H.Q.25th Divisional Train and R.T.O. at Doullens and Candas to make arrangements re train. Fine day but dull.	
"	25th.		87th Brigade moved to Amplier with No. 3 Company. Captain Viveash and 2 N.C.O's proceeded to Doullens to entrain. Arranged with 25th Divisional Train to take over details of H.Q.Coy. and feeding of R.A. 25th Division took over dumps. 87th Brigade with No.3 Company went to Amplier. Pozieres captured. Fine day but dull.	
"	26th.		Visited Companies and D.H.Q. Everything in order. S.S.O. left in evening for North. Fine day but dull till evening.	
"	27th.		Division started moving. Arranged to leave details H.Q.Coy. at Vauchelles for R.A.29th Divisional Train. Trench Mortar Batteries very badly off for Transport. Dull and misty. March with Hdqrs.Train and Hdqrs.of No. 1 Company under Lieut.Blount to Beauval.	
"	28th.		Entrained H.Q.Coy. Section at Candas. Proceeded with Car to Hazebrouck and Poperinghe. Detrained H.Q.Section at Houpoutre. Visited D.H.Q. and Companies. Saw O.C.6th Divl.Train re taking over billets. S.S.O. very busy taking over from S.S.O.6th Division. Very fine day. Division finished moving. Guards Division moving out.	
"	29th.		Poperinghe must be put out of bounds for Divl.Train. Far too many estaminets. 88th Bde. taking over line in Salient. Visited D.D.S & T. 2nd Army.	
POPERINGHE.	"	30th.	86th Bde.moved to Poperinghe. No. 2 Coy.took over camp of No. 4 Coy. 6th Division. Baggage Sections moved to G.A.A.	

2449 Wt. W4957/Mpo 750,000 1/16 J.B.C. & A. Forms/C.2118/12.

WAR DIARY
or
INTELLIGENCE SUMMARY

(Erase heading not required.)

Army Form C. 2118.

Place	Date	Hour	Summary of Events and Information	Remarks and references to Appendices
POPERINGHE	July 31st.		Arranged all the Train Camps and Baggage Sections Lines at EDWAARTHOEK. New system and ought to be good improvement. Visited 6th Divisional Train H.Q. and save animals. Inspected several Refilling Points and made some and took over certain equipment. valuable observations. Hdqrs. of Hd.Qr.Coy.moved to new Camp. Very fine day.	

T.B.Afr.
Lieut.-Col. ASC.
Commdg. 29th Divisional Train.

Army Form C. 2118.

WAR DIARY
or
INTELLIGENCE SUMMARY

(Erase heading not required.)

Instructions regarding War Diaries and Intelligence Summaries are contained in F. S. Regs., Part II. and the Staff Manual respectively. Title Pages will be prepared in manuscript.

Place	Date	Hour	Summary of Events and Information	Remarks and references to Appendices
POPERINGHE.	August 1st.		Headquarters 29th Division moved to Switch Road. 6th Division leaving. Took over the Sanitary fatigues for Poperinghe. 3 Wagons detailed daily for Div.Canteen. Very hot.	
Proven Road.	" 2nd.		Train moved from Poperinghe to Proven Road (late Hdqrs.6th Divl.Train). S.S.O. taking over forward dumps. Very hot.	
"	" 3rd.		Major Jackson inspected 86th First Line Transport. Copes of report to D.H.Q. and Hdqrs.86th Bde. Visited D.H.Q. Welsh Division 113th Bde.arrived. No. 3 and 4 Companies moved into new camp vacated by 6th Division. Sunny and hot.	
"	" 4th.		Went round 1st Line Transport Lines of 86th Bde. with A.A.& Q.M.G. Went to Hdqrs.2nd Army with Adjutant re returns etc. 2 Companies Pioneers(Welsh)and 2 Companies (13th and 14th R.W.F.) attached. Fine day but very dusty.	
"	" 5th.		Adjutant proceeded to 2nd Army Hdqrs. re returns. Prepared estimates for Winter Quarters.	
"	" 6th.		Prepared estimates for material for Winter Quarters. Fine day.	
"	" 7th.		Went round 1st Line Transport and Baggage Sections. Work started, shortage of labour. Front very quiet intermittent shelling by us. Dull day, colder.	
"	" 8th.		1 Wagon to Entrenching Battn. Gas Attack. 2 Horses killed and 2 men slightly gassed. Dr.Newton Hdqr.Coy. displayed great resource in saving his animals. Very hot, harve st well started.	
"	" 9th.		1 Wagon to Anzac Mounted Troops. G.O.C.inspected Lines. Complained of poor condition of horses, pointed out that the work on Somme was more than sufficient to pull them down. Roads started in New Camp. Very hot.	
"	" 10th.		2 Horses on loan to Reserve Company. Went round first line Transport Lines, little progress. Visited Baggage Sections and D.H.Q. Very hot.	

Army Form C. 2118.

WAR DIARY
or
INTELLIGENCE SUMMARY

(Erase heading not required.)

Instructions regarding War Diaries and Intelligence Summaries are contained in F. S. Regs., Part II. and the Staff Manual respectively. Title Pages will be prepared in manuscript.

Place	Date	Hour	Summary of Events and Information	Remarks and references to Appendices
PROVEN ROAD.	August 11th.		D.D.R. turned up to inspect horses. Visited 1st Line Transport and Baggage Lines. Very windy and dusty.	
"	12th.	"	9 Horses evacuated. Cautioned Company Officers about more careful grooming. Hot and stuffy.	
"	13th.	"	Very hot and dusty.	
"	14th.	"	Adjutant proceeded to Remounts at Brearde, and brought back 14 L.D.Mules and 14 L.D.Horses. Proceeded to Vauchelles and inspected Hd.Qr.Coy.details; Lines and Horses most satisfactory. Ordered all Cars into Hdqrs. to be quartered. Supply Officer No. 4 Company ordered into Camp.	
"	15th.	"	Cars ordered into Camp to be garraged.	
"	16th.	"	Went to Cassel to 2nd Army. Roads getting on slowly.	
"	17th.	"	Went round the 1st Line Transport and the Baggage Sections. Units getting on with their standings and doing good work. Ordered 4 Lorries to Ypres for bricks etc. 1 diverted by someone. Rain.	
"	18th.	"	Units complain of shortage of material for standings. Major Jackson went round 1st Line Transport. Major Jackson arranged with R.E. for material for Divisional Train. Very wet and roads bad.	
"	19th.	"	Heavy rain during night, roads very bad. Hdqr.Section started making Lines. Sent Van deh Bemden out to Crombeke to arrange for bricks. Capt.Petrocochino evacuated from 87th Field Ambulance.	
"	20th.	"	Drew rubble from Rousebrugge. Hdqr. Coy. stable started. Visited 87th de.Transport Lines, work progressing. Car No. 236 returned from overhauling.	

Army Form C. 2118.

WAR DIARY
or
INTELLIGENCE SUMMARY
(Erase heading not required.)

Instructions regarding War Diaries and Intelligence Summaries are contained in F.S. Regs., Part II. and the Staff Manual respectively. Title Pages will be prepared in manuscript.

Place	Date	Hour	Summary of Events and Information	Remarks and references to Appendices
PROVEN ROAD.	August 21st.		Stabling progressing in Hdqr. Coy. Went round 1st Line Transport. General air amongst them of "Too many cooks". Laid up with chill. Fine day.	
"	22nd.		Bricks from Rousebrugge arrived. (23,000) Supply Office Hut arrived. Still h bed with chill. Fine day.	
"	23rd.		Still laid up. Intermittent Machine Gun fire during night. Fine day, rain during night.	
"	24th.		Saw Postmaster re letters coming direct to Headquarters of Train. D. of V.S. 2nd Army inspected Horses.	
"	25th.		Report sent to A.A.& Q.M.G. re mule alleged to have been galled by No. 2 Coy. 5 Wheelers arrived from Base. 5 Drivers to 88th Field Ambulance.	
"	26th.		Mails coming in more regularly. Rain during night.	
"	27th.		Showery.	
"	28th.		Italy declares War on Germany and Roumania on Austria. Roofing finished on new stable. Very fine day, hot sun.	
"	29th.		Proceeded on leave. Bad thunderstorm from 2.pm. Rain tropical. Cancelled wagons for YPRES.	
"	30th.		Heavy rain all night. Brigade Major 88th Bde. telephoned for Whale Oil. Trenches full of water.	
"	31st.		Arranged exchange of Horses with Hd.Qr.Coy.20th Divisional Train consequent on Artillery Adjustments. Beautiful fine day. Dried all mens clothes. Special issue of Rum authorised for Troops in Trenches.	

N M Cawthorn
Major for O.C.
29th Divisional Train   ASC.

CONFIDENTIAL.

WAR DIARY OF

29TH DIVISIONAL TRAIN A.S.C.

FROM SEPTEMBER 1st 1916 TO SEPTEMBER 30th 1916.

(VOLUME 7)

xxxxxxxxxxxx

Army Form C. 2118.

WAR DIARY
or
INTELLIGENCE SUMMARY
(Erase heading not required.)

Instructions regarding War Diaries and Intelligence Summaries are contained in F.S. Regs., Part II. and the Staff Manual respectively. Title Pages will be prepared in manuscript.

Place	Date	Hour	Summary of Events and Information	Remarks and references to Appendices
PROVEN ROAD.	Sept.1st.		Exchange of Horses completed. Refilling altered to 10.am. Fine day.	
"	" 2nd.		Visited Bde. Transport Lines and 88th Field Ambulance. Consider progress in erection of Stables and Standings and construction of roads and drains excellent.	
"	" 3rd.		Enemy put 15 shells into Town. Rain during night.	
"	" 4th.		Dull day, Showery.	
"	" 5th.		Returned from leave. Visited Baggage Lines and D.H.Q. Very wet.	
"	" 6th.		Inspected Lines and arranged with O.C.Hd.Qr.Coy. 20th Divisional Train to evacuate 9 complete turnouts. Dr.Candlish run into at level crossing. Fine day and lines drying up.	
"	" 7th.		A.Q.M.G.visited Camps and inspected Standings. Went round Camps with him. Fine day.	
"	" 8th.		O.C.Hd.Qr.Coy. 20th Divisional Train left for South with his Company.	
"	" 9th.		S.S.O. went to meet 29th Divisional Artillery and arrange Supplies. Purchased 3,000 Bricks.	
"	" 10th.		Fine day.	
"	" 11th.		Went to meet 20th Divisional Artillery. Company looking very well. All arrangements most satisfactory. Very fine day. Roofing of Stable completed.	
"	" 12th.		Hd.Qr.Coy. marched in. Orders received for making reductions in Divisional Artillery.	
"	" 13th.		Very wet morning.	
"	" 14th.		Companies busy with Lines. New fatigues for R.E.Works. Fine day.	

2449 Wt. W14957/M90 750,000 1/16 J.B.C. & A. Forms/C.2118/12.

Army Form C. 2118.

WAR DIARY
or
INTELLIGENCE SUMMARY
(Erase heading not required.)

Instructions regarding War Diaries and Intelligence Summaries are contained in F.S. Regs., Part II and the Staff Manual respectively. Title Pages will be prepared in manuscript.

Place	Date	Hour	Summary of Events and Information	Remarks and references to Appendices
PROVEN ROAD.	Sept.15th.		News of fresh advance on the Somme. All Transport to be stopped east of Vlamertinghe after 8.pm. Bombardment at 10.30. Went round Baggage Lines, considerable progress. Rain at night. Sanitary Officer went round Camps, was quite satisfied except Cookhouses, more attention to fly proof meat safes required.	
"	"	16th.	Fine morning.	
"	"	17th.	Went round Wagon Lines and directed improvements. Very wet.	
"	"	18th.	Took Adjutant round Camp and pointed out fresh drainage system. Very wet.	
"	"	19th.	Took Lieut. Macmanaway for interview with A.D. of S. & T. 2nd Army. Very Wet. Drains recut and opened. Camp a swamp. 2 wagons evacuated to R.E. Labour Battalion.	
"	"	20th.	Very wet. Men busy cutting drains. Visited D.H.Q. and Baggage Lines.	
"	"	21st.	Major Jackson visited 2nd Army re establishment. New establishment came in.	
"	"	22nd.	Major Wright reported his arrival and took over command of Hd.Qr.Coy. 16 men including C.Q.M.S. Darley and S.Q.M.S. Acock left for Base.	
"	"	23rd.	Took Major Wright round to D.H.Q. and the Baggage Lines.	
"	"	24th.	Visited D.D.R. D.A.Q.M.G. 29th Division and A.Q.M.G. VIIIth Corps visited lines.	
"	"	25th.	Major Jackson visited Army Headquarters. 5 surplus Wheelers returned to Base.	
"	"	26th.	Visited D.H.Q.	
"	"	27th.	Horse of No. 2 Coy. shot by Anti Aircraft Guns. News received of fall of Thiepval and Combles.	

Army Form C. 2118.

WAR DIARY
or
INTELLIGENCE SUMMARY

(Erase heading not required.)

Instructions regarding War Diaries and Intelligence Summaries are contained in F. S. Regs., Part II. and the Staff Manual respectively. Title Pages will be prepared in manuscript.

Place	Date	Hour	Summary of Events and Information	Remarks and references to Appendices
PROVEN ROAD.	Sept. 28th.		O.C.Hd.Qr.Coy. taking over and certificate posted to 2nd Army. Went round Companies re improvements. Fine day.	
"	29th.		11 Horses arrived for Divisional Train. Surplus men sent to Base under Sgt. Buckingham. Went to Division Hdqrs. to arrange XYZ with S.S.O. Visited 2nd Army re XYZ.	
"	30th.		Visited D.H.Q, Baggage Lines, and Proven Railhead. S.S.O. and A.A.Q.M.G. proceeded by Car to 4th Army Hdqrs with reference to XYZ. XYZ all changed and Railhead not to be changed. Fine day but cold.	

[signature]

Lieut-Col. ASC.
Commdg. 29th Divisional Train.

CONFIDENTIAL.

WAR DIARY OF

29TH DIVISIONAL TRAIN A.S.C.

FROM OCTOBER 1st 1916 TO October 31st 1916.

(VOLUME 8.)

6666666666666666666666666666666666666666666666

Army Form C. 2118.

WAR DIARY
or
INTELLIGENCE SUMMARY
(Erase heading not required.)

Instructions regarding War Diaries and Intelligence Summaries are contained in F. S. Regs., Part II. and the Staff Manual respectively. Title Pages will be prepared in manuscript.

Place	Date		Hour	Summary of Events and Information	Remarks and references to Appendices
PROVEN ROAD.	Oct.	1st.		Balloon set on fire behind 29th front in full view. Very wet.	
"	"	2nd.		Went to Proven re move and also to Wormhoudt. One Brigade arrived of the 55th Division. Very wet.	
"	"	3rd.		Move of 86th postponed 24 hours. O.C.55th Divisional Train went round the Train and was pleased with what he was to take over. Very wet.	
"	"	4th.		Corps Commander inspected the Train and expressed his great satisfaction. Took makeshift Pack Saddles to D.H.Q. Very wet. No. 2 Coy. marched to Wormhoudt and their lines taken over by No. 2 Coy. 55th Divisional Train.	
"	"	5th.		Packing up and handing over. Driver Menton awarded the Military Medal. Fine with showers.	
"	"	6th.		Train Headquarters left for Railway Train. O.C.travelled South in Car via Lillers, St. Poll, Doullens and Amiens. S.S.O. with Gen. Lucas left at 9.am. for Amiens.	
Travelling.	"	7th.		No. 3 Company and No. 4 Company left for South. Arrived Corbie. Billets very congested.	
CORBIE.	"	8th.		Took over from 4th Divisional Train. No. 3 Coy. arrived. Rations late arriving for Mormouths. No. 4 Coy. arrived 24.30. Heavy rain all day.	
"	"	9th.		No. 2 Coy. arrived Daours. Heavy Transport work.	
RIBEMONT.	"	10th.		Headquarters moved to Ribemont. No. 4 Coy. moved to Albert. Fine.	
"	"	11th.		Divisional Headquarters and attached Units Still Ribemont. Went to Railhead Albert. Headquarter Company arrived Daours with R.A. Fine.	
"	"	12th.		Headquarter Coy. moved to A. Camp. R.A. moved to A. Camp. Railhead moved to Albert. Transport very heavy, horses feeling strain and going off in condition. Capt. Simey struck off strength. Apptd. A.P.M. 6th Division.	

2449 Wt. W14957/M90 750,000 1/16 J.B.C. & A. Forms/C.2118/12.

Army Form C. 2118.

WAR DIARY
or
INTELLIGENCE SUMMARY

(Erase heading not required.)

Instructions regarding War Diaries and Intelligence Summaries are contained in F. S. Regs., Part II. and the Staff Manual respectively. Title Pages will be prepared in manuscript.

Place	Date	Hour	Summary of Events and Information	Remarks and references to Appendices
RIBEMONT	Oct. 13th.		Trains very late. 86th and 87th Brigades moved to Fricourt & Mametz Railhead. 14 hours late.	
"	" 14th.		Very late Railhead. 15 hours late. Visited 87th Brigade.	
"	" 15th.		Trains again very late. Refilling better. Went to 4th Army. Wet.	
"	" 16th.		Very late Railhead. 2/Lieut.Purefoy evacuated to England. Capt.G.E.Browne arrived.	
"	" 17th.		Went to Pommier with O.C.No. 2 Company. Railhead very late owing to nonarrival of Train. Capt.Browne took over S.O. 87th Bde.	
"	" 18th.		Moved to E.10 Central. Train at Railhead late again. Very wet.	
E.10. Central.	" 19th.		Ration wagons of 87th Bde. very late returning from Units, having been taken past 1st Line. Complaint sent in to D.H.Q. D.H.Q.moved to Pommier. Late drawing from Railhead owing to refilling being early. D. of T. inspected Train. 87th and 86th Brigades moved into the line. Very wet. Telephoned to D.H.Q. at 6.pm.	
"	" 20th.		Capt.Franks took over Divisional Troops. Lieut.King. took over 88th Bde. Refilling at 12. Railhead at 8.30. ½ hour late. Fine, but cold. Telephoned D.H.Q. at 11.am.	
"	" 21st.		Lieut.Nightingale returned to Base. 1 complete turnout evacuated to 19th Cheshires. 1 wagon evacuated to H.A.G. (62). Very cold, but fine. West Riding R.E. rationed to 22nd. at 5.am. Wagons and horses out all night through their new location not being notified.	
"	" 22nd.		Baggage wagons nearly all returned. Frosty. Fine day.	
"	" 23rd.		A.A.& Q.M.G. visited Camp. Evacuation of 3 surplus complete turnouts to Abbeville. 2 wagons only to 4th Division A.C. 3 surplus men to 88th Field Ambulance. Train very late. All Baggage wagons returned. Frosty. Fine day.	

2449 Wt. W14957/M90 750,000 1/16 J.B.C. & A. Forms/C.2118/12.

Army Form C. 2118.

WAR DIARY
or
INTELLIGENCE SUMMARY

(Erase heading not required.)

Instructions regarding War Diaries and Intelligence Summaries are contained in F. S. Regs., Part II. and the Staff Manual respectively. Title Pages will be prepared in manuscript.

Place	Date	Hour	Summary of Events and Information	Remarks and references to Appendices
E.10. Central.	Oct. 24th.		1 wagon evacuated to 4th D.A.C. Whale Oil and Bicycle Oil sent to 87th Bde. Very wet and damp. Last surplus man evacuated to Base.	
"	" 25th.		Division Canteen Cart finished. Enemy shelling Dernancourt.	
"	" 26th.		News of Verdun success. Very wet.	
"	" 27th.		Began to clear. 88th Bde. Company complaining of the heavy roads and tracks. Difficulty of getting Coke and Charcoal. Visited 4th Army and Corps Hdqrs. re fuel. Wagon evacuated to 56th Divisional Train.	
"	" 28th.		Charcoal satisfactory. Warning received of move. 4 Horses (3 evacuated and 1 dead) O.C. 2nd Australian Divisional Train called. Fine day.	
"	" 29th.		Division coming out of the line.	
"	" 30th.		D.H.Q. moved to Corbie. S.A.A. moved to E.10. Central. 86th Bde. moved to Ville. Very wet, poured all night.	
"	" 31st.		88th Bde. moved to Ville. No. 2 Coy. moved to Corbie. Visited 14th Corps with D.A.Q.M.G.	

Signed, Lieut-Col. ASC.
Commdg. 39th Divisional Train.

CONFIDENTIAL.

WAR   DIARY   OF

29TH   DIVISIONAL   TRAIN   A.S.C.

FROM   NOVEMBER 1st 1916 to NOVEMBER 3oth 1916.

(VOLUME 9.)

-x-x-x-x-x-x-x-x--x-x-x-x-x-x-x-x-x-x-x-x-x-x-xx-x-x-x

Army Form C. 2118.

WAR DIARY
or
INTELLIGENCE SUMMARY

(Erase heading not required.)

Instructions regarding War Diaries and Intelligence Summaries are contained in F. S. Regs., Part II. and the Staff Manual respectively. Title Pages will be prepared in manuscript.

Place	Date	Hour	Summary of Events and Information	Remarks and references to Appendices
CORBIE.	NOVEMBER 1st.		Headquarters of Train moved to Corbie. Good Billets. Fine till afternoon. Shortage of coal.	
"	2nd.		No.3 Coy. moved to Corbie under orders of 87th Bde, orders should have come to me. Visited E.10. Central to see Headquarter Company. Coal supply better. Very wet.	
"	3rd.		20 horses arrived Edgehill. 87th Bde. less Transport move to Airaines with Supply Detachment.	
"	4th.		No. 2 Coy. moved to Brickyard. Fine day.	
"	5th.		No. 3 Coy. moved to Brickyard. Visited 87th Bde. and Abbeville. No. 4 Coy. started to draw from Railhead. Fine day.	
"	6th.		Visited No. 4 and No. 1 Companies and tried to get to Carnoy, but roads blocked with Transport. Shortage of Hay, only 8lbs per horse coming up. Fine day.	
"	7th.		Visited 1 and 2 Companies. Refilling Point much improved and trains more punctual. Wet.	
"	8th.		F.G.C.M. on C.Q.M.S.Kearns. Very wet.	
"	9th.		No. 2 and 3 Companies getting on with lines. Visited No. 4 Company at Mericourt. Fine.	
"	10th.		Amiens bombed. Visited Headquarter Company and sentence on C.Q.M.S.Kearns promulgated. Cpl. Kearns left for Base. Competition between Companies in general turnout. D.A.Q.M.G. and A.D.V.S. judged and awarded to No. 2 Company. A very fine turnout and reflected great credit on all.	
"	11th.		Witness on Court Martial on Bombardier Beasley at E.11 Central. Visited H.Q.Coy. and started threshing straw at Treux. Fine.	

Army Form C. 2118.

WAR DIARY
or
INTELLIGENCE SUMMARY

(Erase heading not required.)

Instructions regarding War Diaries and Intelligence Summaries are contained in F. S. Regs., Part II. and the Staff Manual respectively. Title Pages will be prepared in manuscript.

Place	Date	Hour	Summary of Events and Information	Remarks and references to Appendices
CORBIE.	NOVEMBER 12th.	"	Went to Carnoy and Mericourt to see 8th Divisional Train. Mud awful. Misty and damp.	
"	13th.	"	Conference at D.H.Q. Beaumont Hamel captured. Misty and damp.	
"	14th.	"	No. 3 Coy. moved to E.10 Central and 87th Bde. to Citadel by Bus.	
"	15th.	"	No. 4 Coy. moved to E.10 Central and Bde. to Sandpits. Hdqrs. of Train moved to Treux. Little or no accommodation. Threshing going on steadily. Bombed at night.	
TREUX.	16th.	"	Visited threshing. A great success. No. 2 Coy. moved to Meaulte. Fine and frosty.	
A. 15 C.	17th.	"	Hdqrs. of Train moved to A.15 C. also 3 and 4 Companies. Camp shelled.	
"	18th.	"	Snowed during night and turned to rain, result indescribable mud. S.S.O. sick and ordered to bed.	
"	19th.	"	Transport becoming very difficult and horses felling it. Heavy shelling all night. Very wet.	
"	20th.	"	1st Line ordered to draw from Refilling Point. Work very heavy. Started R.E. work. Fetched Charcoal and Coal from GroveTown. Aeroplanes bombed Camp during night. Several shells into Railhead. Rained all night.	
"	21st.	"	Started making Courdouroy road. Heavy shelling all night. Loading up heavy stocks of fuel. 20 wagons on R.E. work. Shelling all night round Camp and Railhead. Fine, but damp.	
"	22nd.	"	24 wagons of 20th Divisional Train reported. 40 wagons on R.E. work. Fine day. Straw coming in well. Oats short from Railhead supplemented by Cav. Sup. Park. Brought solified Petrol from XIV Corps Dump. Quiet night. Heavy field gun barrage on German counterattack.	

2449 Wt. W14957/M90 750,000 1/16 J.B.C. & A. Forms/C.2118/12.

Army Form C. 2118.

WAR DIARY
or
INTELLIGENCE SUMMARY

(Erase heading not required.)

Instructions regarding War Diaries and Intelligence Summaries are contained in F. S. Regs., Part II. and the Staff Manual respectively. Title Pages will be prepared in manuscript.

Place	Date	Hour	Summary of Events and Information	Remarks and references to Appendices
A.15 C.	NOVEMBER 23rd.		Heavy bomb dropped by aeroplane in Camp. 30 wagons on R.E. work. Shelling during day. Great difficulty with coal. Adjutant very seedy.	
"	24th.		R.E. work telling on horses. Intermittent shelling. Coal difficulties on the increase. Very wet.	
"	25th.		Rained heavily all day. Hd.Qr.Coy. of 4th Division moved out of camp. Shelling Maricourt, one over into camp. Capt Crone arrived.	
"	26th.		Fine after very wet night. Shelling Railhead heavily. 6 Remounts arrived. Visited Hd.Qr.Coy. with M.O. and V.O. Capt.Franks proceeded on special leave.	
"	27th.		Fine day with frost. Lorries arrived Fricourt with straw difficulties re transport. Went to Daours to give lecture on "Supplies in the Field."	
"	28th.		Returned to Camp. Fuel very short. Very cold and damp. Hd.Qr.Coy. ordered to move.	
"	29th.		Hd.Qr.Coy. moved from E.10 Central to Carnoy. Very bad approaches to Camp. Transport very heavy. Keen frost at night. Coal from Edgehill arrived by wagon about 9 also Iron Rations from Fricourt Circus sent there by lorry from 9th Reserve Park.	
"	30th.		Fuel coming in well, but soon issued. Monsieur Rossat went to the trenches as Liason Officer. Adjutant returned to duty.	

[signature]
Lieut-Col. ASC.
Commdg. 29th Divisional Train.

Vol 10

CONFIDENTIAL.

WAR   DIARY   OF

29TH   DIVISIONAL   TRAIN   A.S.C.

FROM DECEMBER 1st 1916 to DECEMBER 31st 1916.

(VOLUME 10.)

XXXXXXXXXXXXXXXXXXXXXXXXXXXXXXXXXXXXXXXXX

Army Form C. 2118.

WAR DIARY
or
INTELLIGENCE SUMMARY

(Erase heading not required.)

Instructions regarding War Diaries and Intelligence Summaries are contained in F. S. Regs., Part II. and the Staff Manual respectively. Title Pages will be prepared in manuscript.

Place	Date	Hour	Summary of Events and Information	Remarks and references to Appendices
A.15 c.	DECEMBER 1st.		S.S.O. and Major Wright visited 4th Army. Fuel coming in better. Frosty.	
"	2nd.		Daimler Car's radiator froze and sent into Supply Column. 86th Brigade complained about Preserved Meat. Unavoidable owing to Port of Havre closed. Dull and cold.	
"	3rd.		S.S.O. and Adjutant 20th Division arrived to look round. Coal wagons returned empty from Edgehill. Interpreter Rossat returned.	
"	4th.		Visited all Brigade Headquarters with S.S.O. also Divisional Headquarters. Fine day and sunny.	
"	5th.		Nothing important. Fine.	
"	6th.		Made arrangements re move. Fine.	
"	7th.		Visited Headquarter Company with Medical Officer. New Warrant Officer and C.Q.M.S. arrived as reinforcements. Fine.	
"	8th.		Visited new area. Went to lunch with General Carter. Came back through Amiens. Car broke down. Lieut. Hunt took over 14th Corps Troops as Supply Officer. Very wet.	
"	9th.		87th Brigade move to Ville. Brigade Company of 20th Divisional Train arrived. Aeroplanes dropped several bombs on Railhead. Heavy aeroplane fighting during the night. Heavy rain all day.	
"	10th.		Companies move to E.10 Central. S.S.O. moved to Corbie. 2 Brigade Companies of 20th Divisional Train moved in. Railhead, Edgehill.	
"	11th.		Railhead heavily bombed and anti-aircraft very busy during the night. Hdqrs. Train moved to Corbie. 87th Brigade less Headquarters moved to Corbie. Raining.	

Army Form C. 2118.

WAR DIARY
or
INTELLIGENCE SUMMARY

(Erase heading not required.)

Instructions regarding War Diaries and Intelligence Summaries are contained in F. S. Regs., Part II. and the Staff Manual respectively. Title Pages will be prepared in manuscript.

Place	Date	Hour	Summary of Events and Information	Remarks and references to Appendices
CORBIE.	DECEMBER 12th.		Divisional Headquarters moved to Corbie. 87th Brigade moved to new area. Nos. 2 and 3 Companies moved to new area. Raining.	
"	13th.		Train Headquarters left Corbie for Oissy. Nos. 2 and 3 Companies arrived in new area.	
OISSY.	14th.		Visited Nos. 2 and 3 Companies also No. 3 Company's Refilling Point. Visited B.H.Q. Major Wright arrived.	
"	15th.		Conference at D.H.Q.16.30.a.m. Col. Sykes proceeded on leave to England.	
"	16th.		Visited Nos. 2, 3 and 4 Companies also No. 3 Company's Refilling Point. Orders recived for Companies to move as under on the 18th instant. No. 2 Coy. to Ailly. No. 3 Coy. to Crouy. No. 4 Coy. to Dreuil-les-Molliens.	
"	17th.		Visited Headquarter Company and Detachment at Plateau. Saw D.D.S & T. re Major Gillem's application, also supply of wood for Divisional Artillery, which is to be drawn from 14th Corps Fuel Dump. Sgt.Stanley brought to Train Headquarters for temporary duty in Office.	
"	18th.		Companies moved as under:- No. 2 Coy. from Pourdrinay to Ailly. No. 3 Coy. " Picquigny to Crouy. No. 4 Coy. " Camps-en-Amienois to Dreuil-les-Molliens. Brought Car in from Headquarter Company owing to breakdown of 2nd Vauxhall Car. Sent for 2 Clipping Machines from Headquarter Company. Visited No. 4 Coy. after their move also D.S.C. with Adjutant.	
"	19th.		Sadd,S.Q.M.S.Acock joined from 49th (W.R.) Divl.Train and posted to No. 4 Coy. Authority:- D.A.G.Base, wire ST.8347 dated 13.12.16. Issued 1 Machine Clipper to each of No. 3 and 4 Companies. Visited No. 3 Coy. and inspected stabling and billets. Visited No. 2 Coy. Arrangements for refilling.G.dump supplies for 86th and 87th Bdes. at Ailly and Crouy respectively, delivery to Units being made by supply wagons. Supplies for 88th Bde. dumped at top of hill ¼ mile S.W. of Picquigny on road to Cavillon, where they are picked up by supply wagons and taken to 88th Bde. Dump at Dreuil-les-Molliens, thence by 1st Line transport to Units.	

2449 Wt. W14957/M90 750,000 1/16 J.B.C. & A. Forms/C.2118/12.

Army Form C. 2118.

WAR DIARY
or
INTELLIGENCE SUMMARY

(Erase heading not required.)

Instructions regarding War Diaries and Intelligence Summaries are contained in F. S. Regs., Part II. and the Staff Manual respectively. Title Pages will be prepared in manuscript.

Place	Date	Hour	Summary of Events and Information	Remarks and references to Appendices
ISSY.	DECEMBER 20th.		Lieut.Hunt ordered to report to 14th Corps Supply Column as Corps Fuel Officer. Following transfers made. Capt.Browne to Supply Officer 86th Brigade. Lieut.King to Supply Officer 87th Brigade. Visited No. 3 Company's Refilling Point during refilling. Inspected No. 4 Company's Stables and Billets. Capt.Upson to Paris on 48 hours leave. Frost.	
"	21st.		7 wagons under Lieut.Goodman detailed to draw fuel wood from BOIS DE NEUILLY to roadway where it is picked up in lorries and taken to Brigade Dumps. Some difficulty in getting lorries or fatigue party to load. Straw delivered from FERRIERES to Brigade Dumps by Lorries.	
"	22nd.		Wagons from Lieut.Blount draw wood from BOIS DE NEUILLY to roadside. Accompanied S.S.O. to each Brigade Dump and Railhead. Accompanied Major Gillam to Divisional School,DAOURS, where he gave a lecture on Supplies.	
"	23rd.		Ordered to draw from Railhead –HANGEST– by Horse Transport from tomorrow. Made following arrangement with D.A.Q.M.G. to take effect tomorrow. No. 2 Coy. Lorries continue to deliver to Ailly. No. 3 Coy. Issue rations for consumption 25th inst. by Supply wagons which proceed to Hangest and draw supplies for consumption 26th inst. No. 4 Coy. Lorries deliver Supplies for consumption 25th inst which are drawn from Refilling Point by 1st Line Transport. Supply wagons draw supplies for consumption 26th instant from Railhead and convey to Refilling Point for 1st line to draw.	
"	24th.		Inspected No. 2 Company with Adjutant. Railhead changed to Hangest.	
"	25th.		Visited all Companies with Adjutant. S.S.O. makes following arrangements for supply of fuel wood. He proposes to buy a considerable quantity of tools for felling, and has made arrangements with the owner of a Bois near MOLLIENS-VIDAME to cut trees there, using Newfoundland men for the work. Would this timber be fit to use immediately as fuel? Very doubtful. It would be a good plan, if each Division, when in rest, regularly cut a supply of timber for use some months ahead.	

Army Form C. 2118.

WAR DIARY
or
INTELLIGENCE SUMMARY
(Erase heading not required.)

Instructions regarding War Diaries and Intelligence Summaries are contained in F. S. Regs., Part II. and the Staff Manual respectively. Title Pages will be prepared in manuscript.

Place	Date	Hour	Summary of Events and Information	Remarks and references to Appendices
OISSY	DECEMBER 26th.		Capt. Bell proceeded to Junior Staff College, Hesdin. Capt. Upson ordered to take over Supply Officer, Divisional Troops. Saw D.A.D.S. re wood question, awaiting instructions from Corps regarding purchase of saws, axes, etc. for fellers. Went to Poudrigney with Capt. Franks to see what straw was available for issue tomorrow - find about 6 loads. Warmer says that most of the Straw has been bespoken by a following Division. Sgt Capt. Browne to see Garde des Bois at BOIS de NEUILLY. He reports that we can obtain 35 tons brushwood daily for an unlimited period, if we supply labour to lop the trees which have already been felled for French Government. Made arrangements with "Q" to commence work on 28th with 50 men.	
"	27th.		Corps refuse authority to purchase tools for weed cutting. Returned off leave and reassured Command. Inspected No. 4 Company and found the waggons harness and horses in a very indifferent state. Frosty.	
"	28th.		Thaw all day. Car No. 238 returned from Workshops. Railhead very late. Train did not arrive till 1.40. Thursday morning.	
"	29th.		Horses getting in a low state owing to hard work and short forage. Arranged that Supply Column should draw from Railhead to relieve No. 4 Company.	
"	30th.		Visited 4th Army with S.S.O. Saw D.D. of R. and D.D.S & T. S.S.O. arranged fatigue party for cutting wood. Major Wright inspected No. 3 Company. Horse question becoming acute.	
"	31st.		Went round Farms to try and purchase hay but none available owing to previous purchase of French and English.	

[signature] Lieut-Col. ASC.
Commdg. 29th Divisional Train ASC.

CONFIDENTIAL.

WAR DIARY OF
29TH DIVISIONAL TRAIN A.S.C.
FROM JANUARY 1st 1917 to JANUARY 31st 1917.
(VOLUME 11.)
XXXXXXXXXXXXXXXXXXXXXXXXXX

Army Form C. 2118.

WAR DIARY
or
INTELLIGENCE SUMMARY

(Erase heading not required.)

Instructions regarding War Diaries and Intelligence Summaries are contained in F. S. Regs., Part II. and the Staff Manual respectively. Title Pages will be prepared in manuscript.

Place	Date	Hour	Summary of Events and Information	Remarks and references to Appendices
OISSY.	Jan. 1st.	17..	Went round 3t. 2 Coys. 2 Good. 3 Bad. Inspected No. 4 Coy. Good. Went to Molliens Vidame Wood to see wooducutting. Artillery change Railhead. No news given officially. Went out to Meaulte did not return till 4-30 a.m..	
	" 2nd.		New leave allotment. Major Wright visited Plateau and H.Q. Coy. and Corps and Army H.Q. and smoothed out a general muddle and obtained a promise of horses.	
	" 3rd.		Wire received that Baggage wagons will return and have left Plateau at 11a.m. Visited wood cutting. Also 3 and 2 Coys.	
	" 4th.		Horses and wagons under Capt Crone have arrived from Plateau. Horses very thin. Visited wood cutting which is getting better organised.	
	" 5th.		Horses arrived from Base. 34 H.D. and 2 Riders. Went to Army and H.Q. Coy and arranged with D.D.S.T. about 30 tons of coal being sent to E. 22. C.	
	" 6th.		First orders of move received. Visited Coys. and saw remounts, very pleased with stamp of Remounts.	
	" 7th.		Nothing of importance. Went round Coys with A.D.V.S. who was pleased with condition of animals.	
	" 8th.		Went round Coys. Wood cutting finished. Orders very late owing to late arrival of Divl. Orders. Orders issued to Coys re march. Snow and rain.	
	" 9th.		4 Horses to 89th. Field Ambulance. Visited D.H.Q. and 2 & 3 Coys.	
	" 10th.		86th. Brigade moved to Corbie, and No. 2 Coy.	
Corbie.	" 11th.		No.4 Coy and 88th. Bde. march to Corbie. No. 2 Coy and 86th. Bde. march to Meaulte and Ville. H.Q. of Train and Divl. H.Q. arrived at Corbie.	
	" 12th.		No. 3 Coy and 87th. Bde. march to Bresle. Visited H.Q. 17th. Divl. Train to make	

Army Form C. 2118.

WAR DIARY
or
INTELLIGENCE SUMMARY
(Erase heading not required.)

Instructions regarding War Diaries and Intelligence Summaries are contained in F. S. Regs., Part II. and the Staff Manual respectively. Title Pages will be prepared in manuscript.

Place	Date	Hour	Summary of Events and Information	Remarks and references to Appendices
CORBIE.	Jan 12th.		arrangements about taking over.	
"	13th.		Brigades moving up peacemeal. Very difficult grouping Units owing to lack of information. R.E. & R.A.M.C. especially bad owing to constant changing of locations. 5 Remounts arrived drawn by H.Q. Coy in a very bad condition.	
"	14th.		Nothing of importance happened.	
A. 15. C.	15th.		Train H.Q. and No. 4 coy, moved from Corbie to Plateau. Guard placed at Maricourt Bois. Arrangements for meeting Reinforcements and leave Trains arranged. Very cold and Bitter winds.	
"	16th.		D.H.Q. and remainder of 88th. moved to forward Area. Railhead at 7- 30 a.m. and H.Q. Coy at 1 p.m. Hard frost and very cold. Snow and roads very bad. Ordered frost cogs to be put on the horses feet.	
"	17th.		S.S.O. visited 6th. Army D.D.S.T. to clear up Supply matters. S.O. H.Q. Coy especially to blame also S.O. S.C., but no reflection on the present S.O.	
"	18th.		Met A.A.& Q.M.G. AND WENT TO LOOK AT Maricourt Bois. Settled to send No. 3 Coy to prepare Camp.	
"	19th.		Major Wright took over S.S.O. of Division. Took O.C. No. 3 Coy to look at Maricourt Bois. Very cold and keen frost.	
"	20th.		No. 3. Coy left for Maricourt Bois. S.S.O. left for leave via Paris.	
"	21st.		Nothing to report.	
"	22nd.		Lt. Cowans attached for duty. Maricourt Bois road improving. Thaw rations issued.	
"	23rd.		Inspected 1stl Line Transport. Remainder of Thaw Rations issued. Started sick lines at Maricourt. S.S.O. went to Guillemont to B.H.Q. Bitterly cold and severe frost.	
"	24th.		Lecture on Supplies at Daours. Adjutant took 24 S.O.S. Rifle Grenades to Ginchy.	
"	24th.			

Army Form C. 2118.

WAR DIARY
or
INTELLIGENCE SUMMARY

(Erase heading not required.)

Instructions regarding War Diaries and Intelligence Summaries are contained in F. S. Regs., Part II. and the Staff Manual respectively. Title Pages will be prepared in manuscript.

Place	Date	Hour	Summary of Events and Information	Remarks and references to Appendices
A. 15. c.	Jan. 25th.		Inspected 1st. Line Transport. Coal coming in very badly. Very cold but fine.	
"	26th.		Inspected 1st. Line Transport. Went to consult O.C. Train 20th. Div. re working parties for Maricourt Bois. Very cold and hard frost continues.	
"	27th.		Visited D.H.Q. Daimler cracked radiator pipe. Attack on salient in front of Le. Transloy about 400 prisoners. Extremely cold.	
"	28th.		No. 2 Coy. moved to Maricourt Bois. Very cold.	
"	29th.		Fuel very scarce none coming up, telephoned D.D.S.T. Drew from Corps Dump. Lt. Cowans left Train for D.H.Q. Q.M.S. Meagher reported for duty with D.H.Q. Visited 17th. Train. Very cold.	
"	30th.		Fuel getting a serious position, Division, Corps, and Army informed. S.S.O. went to Accounts Branch and Army. Visited 1st. Line Transport. D.A.Q.M.G. called. Very cold and snowing all day.	
"	31st.		No relief in the Fuel scarcity. Visited 1st. Line Transport. Lieut. Macmanaway went to Edgehill on duty. Very cold and slippery no sign of Thaw.	

Lieut. Col, A.S.C.

Commdg. 29th. Divisional Train.

CONFIDENTIAL

WAR DIARY OF

29th. DIVISIONAL TRAIN A.S.C.

FROM FEBRUARY 1st to FEBRUARY 28th. 1917

(VOLUME 12)

Army Form C. 2118.

WAR DIARY
or
INTELLIGENCE SUMMARY

(Erase heading not required.)

Instructions regarding War Diaries and Intelligence Summaries are contained in F. S. Regs., Part II. and the Staff Manual respectively. Title Pages will be prepared in manuscript.

Place	Date	Hour	Summary of Events and Information	Remarks and references to Appendices
A.15.c.	Feb. 1st.		Nothing of importance. Very cold.	
"	2nd.		Visited 4th Army, 20th Divisional Train H.Q., 34th D.S.C. and D.D.R. Obtained 20 tons of coal, 5 tons straw and six horses.	
"	3rd.		Fuel very scarce. Went to FROISSY to see Canal arrangements. Very cold, thermometer below zero.	
"	4th.		Move table came and regrouping completed by 11 p.m. Went to 20th Div. Train re taking over.	
"	5th.		S.S.C. returned off Leave. Fuel very scarce. All cars broken down, wired to 34th D.S.C. push on with repairs. Very cold. Enemy aeroplane bombed camps, 52 horses 17th Bde. R.A. killed, and wounded, 8 horses 8th Staffords killed.	
"	6th		Major Gilter went with S.S.O. 17th Division to Accounts Branch. Arranged to draw four Nissen Huts for Division. NO 2 Coy. left for LA NEUVILLE, NO. 4 Coy left for CARDONNETTE via BONNAY. Very cold. Lieut. Goodman joined Agricultural Board.	
"	7th.		NO. 3 Coy left for MEAULTE. Railhead heavily shelled. Reinforcement Hut blown up also Corps postal hut, six men wounded. 20th Divisional Train took over. Fuel for Thaw Rations came in, completed by 9 p.m.	
HEILLY.	8th		Train H.Q. moved to HEILLY.	
"	9th.		Arranged wood cutting. H.Q. of Division arrived.	
"	10th		Coal train arrived 24 hours late. Went round Railhead, Field Supply Depot, 86th & 87th Dumps with S.S.O.	
"	11th		Nothing of importance.	
"	12th		Inspected 87th Bde 1st Line.	
"	13th		Started drawing by H.T. for No. 2 Group. Inspected 86th Bde 1st Line. Capt. Upson went to Paris.	
"	14th.		Inspected 88th. Bde 1st Line. Capt. Browne went on Leave on urgent private affairs.	

Army Form C. 2118.

WAR DIARY
or
INTELLIGENCE SUMMARY
(Erase heading not required.)

Instructions regarding War Diaries and Intelligence Summaries are contained in F. S. Regs., Part II. and the Staff Manual respectively. Title Pages will be prepared in manuscript.

Place	Date	Hour	Summary of Events and Information	Remarks and references to Appendices
Heilly.	Feb. 15th.		O.C. 17th Divisional Train visited re move. Received move orders from Division.	
"	16th.		Coal Train arrived 50 tons for 29th Division. Ammunition Dump Plateau blown up. One man and one horse wounded, one horse killed. S.S.O. and Adjutant getting out orders for move.	
"	17th.		H.Q. Coy Supply Section moved to E. 22. c. Great delay in getting out orders. S.S.O. out all night putting matters straight.	
"	18th		Orders altered and very late. No. 4 Coy moved to E. 22. c. Advance party of No. 3 Coy. went to Plateau.	
"	19th.		Railhead for two Bdes. at Plateau. Railhead for 86th at Mericourt. No. 2 Coy moved to Plateau. No. 3 and 4 Coys. moved to Plateau. Major Wright left on two days leave to Paris.	
Minden Post. "	20th.		H.Q. Divisional Train left for Minden Post.	
"	21st.		Remainder of troops moved to Forward Area. One H.D. horse died from overwork attached 1st Border Regt. Visited Railhead. Started two Group system. S.S.O. visited 4th Army.	
"	22nd.		Capt Bell went to Div.H. Q. Transport very heavy.	
"	23rd		Nothing of importance. One tip cart broken.	
"	24th.		Transport very heavy.	
"	25th		Everything quiet.	
"	26th.		Lecture Divisional School at 6 p.m. Roads from DAOURS and LA NEUVILLE impassable and had to go by way of PONT NOYELLES. General news of advance.	
"	27th		Visited D.H.Q. xxxxxxxxxxxxxxxxxxxxxxxxxx.Roads getting very cut up. No news of move everything still vague. Troops still advancing along the ANCRE.	
"	28th.		Visited D.H.Q. also 17th and Guards Div Trains re move. Roads very bad and cut up by lorries. 60 prisoners taken by 86th Bde. Heavy firing during night apparently in direction of SAILLISEL. Lieut. Macmanaway left for G.H.Q. but car broke down.	

Lt. Col. A.S.C.

2449 Wt. W14957/M90 750,000 1/16 J.B.C. & A. Forms/C.2118/12.

CONFIDENTIAL.

WAR DIARY OF
29th. DIVISIONAL TRAIN A.S.C.
FROM MARCH 1st. to MARCH 31st. 1917.

(VOLUME 13).

Army Form C. 2118.

WAR DIARY
or
INTELLIGENCE SUMMARY

(Erase heading not required.)

Instructions regarding War Diaries and Intelligence
Summaries are contained in F. S. Regs., Part II.
and the Staff Manual respectively. Title Pages
will be prepared in manuscript.

Place	Date	Hour	Summary of Events and Information	Remarks and references to Appendices
MINDEN POST.	March 1st.		March tables very late in arriving. Arranged move.	
"	2nd.		Final arrangements made re move to Reserve Area. Units started moving.	
"	3rd.		All Companies moved, No. 2 Coy - MERICOURT., No. 3 Coy. - LA NEUVILLE., No.4 Coy. - MEAULTE. Informed that D.H.Q. were not moving until the 5th. inst.	
HEILLY.	4th.		3 Brigades Companies drew from MERICOURT. Very wet and roads bad. Lorries being restricted. Moved to HEILLY.	
"	5th.		Visited Nos. 2,3 and 4 Companies, animals looking very fair considering the work. No. 1 Coy. drawing from MARICOURT BOIS.	
"	6th.		Visited Treux Laundry and No. 2 Coy. No. 2 and 4 Groups drawing by H.T. No. 1 Coy. drawing from MERICOURT assisted by Nos. 2 and 4 Companies. Heavy fall of snow during the night.	
"	7th.		Transferred 10 wagons on detail from No. 3 to No. 2 Company. Lorries being very much restricted.	
"	8th.		Visited No. 3 Company. Hard frost, very cold.	
"	9th.		Visited No. 4 Company and No.1 with Adjutant. 1 H.D. Horse destroyed in No. 4 Company. Corrected War Establishments. 120 tons of coal came from CORBIE. Transport work very heavy for Brigade Companies.	
"	10th.		Nothing of importance.	
"	11th.		Nothing to report.	
"	12th.		Major E.T.L.Wright took over temporary duties of Requisitioning Officer. 30 Remounts arrived, not very good. Captain C.E.Browne returned off leave.	
"	13th.		Inspected 86th. Bde. 1st. Line Transport in the morning and 87th. Brigade in the afternoon.	

Army Form C. 2118.

WAR DIARY
or
INTELLIGENCE SUMMARY

(Erase heading not required.)

Instructions regarding War Diaries and Intelligence Summaries are contained in F. S. Regs., Part II. and the Staff Manual respectively. Title Pages will be prepared in manuscript.

Place	Date	Hour	Summary of Events and Information	Remarks and references to Appendices
HEILLY.	March 14th.		Inspected 88th. Bde. 1st. Line Transport. Compiled Historical History of the Train for D.D.S & T. 4th. Army. Captains J.S.Crone and D.P.C Franks proceeded on leave to Paris.	
	" 15th.		Lieut. P.W.T. Mew reported his arrival. Inspected No. 2 Company.	
	" 16th.		Inspected Nos. 1 and 4 Companies.	
	" 17th.		Move of Division ordered to Back Area. Went to CORBIE to see O.C. 33rd. Divisional Train, if they wanted to take over any fuel. BAPAUME taken and Troops advancing on 80 mile front.	
	" 18th.		1st Line of 87th. and 88th. Brigades also No. 3 and 4 Companies moved to Back Area by stages. News received of ROYE and PERONNE having fallen.	
OISSY.	" 19th.		No. 2 Company and 1st. Line moved to Back Area staging at DAOURS. News received of NOYON and NESLES having fallen.	
	" 20th.		Headquarters of Division etc., moved to Back Area. News still coming in of advance.	
	" 21st.		Major E.T.L.Wright proceeded to HEILLY Area re Claims. Visited Nos. 3 and 4 Companies. Artillery came out of Line to MORLANCOURT. Went to AIRAINES re No. 2 Coy. Arrangements made for No. 3 Coy. to go to CONDE.	
	" 22nd.		No. 2 Company drawing from PONT REMY by Horse Transport in order to release Lorries. Adjutant and S.S.O. went to Nos. 2 and 3 Companies to make arrangements re drawing from Railhead by Horse Transport. Captain E.C. Bell and Dr. Smailes and 1 set of saddlery left for 18th. Corps.	
	" 23rd.		No. 3 Company drawing from Railhead to release Lorries.	
	" 24th.		Went round Brigade Companies.	
	" 25th.		Visited 4th. and 5 th. Armies re march, and Headquarter Coy. on the way back.	
	" 26th.		Nothing of importance.	

2449 Wt. W14957/M90 750,000 1/16 J.B.C. & A. Forms/C.2118/12.

Army Form C. 2118.

WAR DIARY
or
INTELLIGENCE SUMMARY

(Erase heading not required.)

Instructions regarding War Diaries and Intelligence Summaries are contained in F. S. Regs., Part II. and the Staff Manual respectively. Title Pages will be prepared in manuscript.

Place	Date	Hour	Summary of Events and Information	Remarks and references to Appendices
OISSY.	March	27th.	Limber sent to Royal Fusiliers. Visited Nos. 2 and 1 Companies. Went to Front Area, roads very bad and impassable in places.	
	"	28th.	Visited Nos. 4 and 3 Companies. Arranged to send harness to Royal Fusiliers.	
VIGNACOURT.	"	29th.	Marched to VIGNACOURT. Major E.T.L.Wright remaining behind to settle claims for Division. Daimler car breaks down and sent to shops. No. 2 Coy. marched to COMME. No. 3 Coy. marched to VIGNACOURT, No. 4 Coy marched to St. Pierre Crouy.	
	"	30th.	Remained at VIGNACOURT. Headquarters of Division marched to VIGNACOURT. No.2 Coy. marched to HALLOY. No. 3 Coy marched to PIEFFES, No. 4 Coy. marched to FIEFFIUES. 7½ tons of Hay drawn from CANDAS.	
BEAUVAL.	"	31st.	Marched to BEAUVAL and stayed the night. Very wet in the evening. Lieut. G.A. Goodman left for 32nd Divisional Train. Lieut R.T.R. Macmanaway went to G.H.Q.	

Lieut. Col. A.S.C.
Commdg 29th Divisional Train.

CONFIDENTIAL.

WAR   DIARY   OF

29th. DIVISIONAL TRAIN A.S.C.

From April 1st.   To April 31st. 1917.

(Volume 14).

Army Form C. 2118.

WAR DIARY
or
INTELLIGENCE SUMMARY.
(Erase heading not required.)

Instructions regarding War Diaries and Intelligence Summaries are contained in F. S. Regs., Part II. and the Staff Manual respectively. Title pages will be prepared in manuscript.

Place	Date	Hour	Summary of Events and Information	Remarks and references to Appendices
BEAUVAL	1-4-17.		Division marched in, staged at Beauval.	
	2-4-17.		The whole Division marched to new Area. Headquarters Divisional Train leaving at 6 a.m. Divisional Headquarters same place. No. 2 Coy. to HALLOY., No. 3 Coy. to Les Callmonts Farm, LUCHEUX., No. 4 Coy. to MONDICOURT.	
	3-4-17.		Divisional Train drew by Horse Transport. Pack train many 24 hours late. 2nd. Lieut. T.G. Mathews reported. Work for horses extremely heavy.	
	4-4-17.		Divisional Train drew by Horse Transport. Train very late.	
BAVINCOURT	5-4-17.		Motor Transport drew from Railhead. Divisional H.Q. and Divisional Train H.Q. moved to BAVINCOURT, No. 2 Coy. to SUS ST. LEGER., No. 3 Coy. to ETREE VAMIN., No. 4 Coy. to IVERGNY. Fine day.	
	6-4-17.		Divisional Train drew by Horse Transport moving after loading, No. 2 to SUS ST. LEGER, No. 3 to WARLUZ., No. 4 Coy. to COUTURELLE. Division remained fast for 24 hours.	
	7-4-17.		No 2 Coy. moved to LAHERLIER., No. 3 Coy. moved to WARLUZ., No. 4 Coy. moved to	
	8-4-17.		No. 3 Coy. moved to BAVINCOURT. Visited No. 4 Coy. Went to ARRAS with S.S.O. to see Dump and roads.	
	9-4-17.		Vimy Ridge captured and 4,000 prisoners. Visited 2 and 4 Companies. Major E.T.L.Wright acting as S.T.O.	
	10-4-17.		No.4 Company went to GOUY. Very squally wet and snowy.	
	11-4-17.		Division in Bavincourt Area.	
AGNEZ	12-4-17.		Divisional Headquarters moved to WAGNONLIEU. Train H.Q. to AGNEZ. No. 2, 3 and 4 Companies moved to DAINVILLE. 88th. Brigade went into Line.	

2353 Wt. W2544/1454 700,000 5/15 D.D. & L. A.D.S.S./Forms/C. 2118.

Army Form C. 2118.

WAR DIARY
or
INTELLIGENCE SUMMARY.
(Erase heading not required.)

Instructions regarding War Diaries and Intelligence Summaries are contained in F. S. Regs., Part II. and the Staff Manual respectively. Title pages will be prepared in manuscript.

Place	Date	Hour	Summary of Events and Information	Remarks and references to Appendices
DAINVILLE	13-4-17.		Divisional Headquarters moved to ARRAS. Train Headquarters moved to DAINVILLE.	
	14-4-17.		Drawing from AGNEZ by Motor Transport. Nos. 2, 3 and 4 Companies moved to CITADELLE. Train Headquarters to ARRAS. Town full of Troops. Fine day.	
ARRAS	15-4-17.		Visited Companies and Divisional Headquarters. Drawing by Motor Transport from ARRAS. Very wet.	
	16-4-17.		Visited D.H.Q.; Railhead and Refilling Points. 3 Bde. Companies moved from Citadelle to St. Quentin Rd. Went with Major E.T.L.Wright to visit S.M.T.O.	
	17-4-17.		Heavy shelling both sides. Visited Companies and Refilling Points. Very wet.	
	18-4-17.		Shelling very heavy. Town main water supply cut by lucky shell. Saw A.A.Q.M.G. Went with A.D.O.S. VI Corps to arrange Salvage Dump and Watering Place for 1st. Line Transport.	
	19-4-17.		Headquarter Company moved to RONVILLE. 6 Limbers for R.E. work. Daimler returned from Workshops.	
	20-4-17.		Went to 3rd. Army H.Q. and saw D.D.S.& T. and also D.D.R. Major E.T.L.Wright handed over Command of No.1 Coy. to Capt. F.M. Upson. Heavy shells on Town intermittently.	
	21-4-17.		Major E.T.L.Wright left to take command of 4th. Reserve Park. 6 H.D.Horses arrived and 1 mule. Town shelled from 3-45 a.m. to 4-15 a.m. Visited Companies.	
	22-4-17.		Heavy bombardment all day and night. Shells dropping in the Town. Fine.	
	23-4-17.		General attack. visited all Companies with A.D.V.S. and selected 11 horses for transfer to Base0.C.Companies reconnoitred side road to Tilloy as an alternative to main Cambrai Road which is under considerable shell fire. Heavy bombardment all night. Very fine.	
BERNEVILLE	24-4-17.		Fine day, moved to BERNEVILLE. Transport looking very well.	

Army Form C. 2118.

WAR DIARY
or
INTELLIGENCE SUMMARY.
(Erase heading not required.)

Instructions regarding War Diaries and Intelligence Summaries are contained in F. S. Regs., Part II. and the Staff Manual respectively. Title pages will be prepared in manuscript.

Place	Date	Hour	Summary of Events and Information	Remarks and references to Appendices
WANQUETIN.	25-4-17.		Moved to Wanquetin via Rosart. Ammunition Dump blown up at ARPAS. Fine day.	
COUIN.	26-4-17.		Moved to COUIN. No. 4 to Couin, No. 3 Company to LAHERLIER., No. 2 Company to SOUASTRE.	
	27-4-17.		Nos. 2 and 3 Companies drew by Horse Transport from Railhead. Visited Companies.	
	28-4-17.		Visited Heberteune, Gommecourt, Pusieux, Miraumont and Beaumont Hamel. Capt. I. Newton reported his arrival.	
	29-4-17.		Nothing of importance.	
	30-4-17.		Visited No. 2 Company. Fine day.	

Lieut. Col. A.S.C.
Commdg. 29th. Divisional Train.

CONFIDENTAL.

WAR DIARY OF
29TH. DIVISIONAL TRAIN A.S.C.
FROM May, 1st.   TO MAY, 31st., 1917.

(VOLUME 15).

Army Form C. 2118.

WAR DIARY
or
INTELLIGENCE SUMMARY.
(Erase heading not required.)

Instructions regarding War Diaries and Intelligence Summaries are contained in F. S. Regs., Part II. and the Staff Manual respectively. Title pages will be prepared in manuscript.

Place	Date	Hour	Summary of Events and Information	Remarks and references to Appendices
COUIN.	1/5/17.		Companies moved. 2 coy. to GOMY with Brigade Groups,3Coy.MANQUETION with Brigade Groups, and 4 Coy. to SAULTY with Brigade Groups. Fine Days.	
ARRAS.	2/5/17.		Companies parked on racecourse ARRAS. Hd.Qrs. moved to Rue des TEINTURIERS. Very fine day and dusty. Div. Hd. Qrs. moved to PXXXXX PLACE ST. CROIX, ARRAS.	
	3/5/17.		87th. went into Support Trenches. Visited Companies with Adjutant. Town shelled badly and two shells pitched into Train Hd. Qrs. killing 4 horses.	
	4/5/17.		Dead horses removed and Train Hd. Qrs. removed to RACECOURSE. Ammunition Dump blown up in ARRAS. Visited III Army Hd. Qrs.	
	5/5/17.		Visited D.H.Q. and all Companies. A.A.& Q.M.G. visited Camp.	
	6/5/17.		Ammunition Dump blown up at St.Saveur and all Transport removed from town. Very fine day.	
	7/5/17		Ammunition Dumps shelled at DAINVILLE and DOULLENS forked road. Reinforcements arrived.Very fine day.	
	8/5/17.		Left RACECOURSE for BERNEVILLE. Wet day. No. 2 Coy. was left at ARRAS, No.3 Coy. moved to DUISANS and No.4 Coy. moved to BERNEVILLE.	
BERNEVILLE.	9/5/17.		Visited D.H.Q. Fine day.	
	10/5/17		Nothing of importance. Fine day.	

Army Form C. 2118.

WAR DIARY
or
INTELLIGENCE SUMMARY.
(Erase heading not required.)

Instructions regarding War Diaries and Intelligence Summaries are contained in F. S. Regs., Part II. and the Staff Manual respectively. Title pages will be prepared in manuscript.

Place	Date	Hour	Summary of Events and Information	Remarks and references to Appendices
BERNEVILLE	11/5/17.		No. 4 Coy. and Bde. Group changed over with 88th. Bde. Group. Fine Day.	
	12/5/17.		Visited Companies. ROEUX village partly captured also BULLECOURT.	
	13/5/17.		Inspected 86th. Bde. First Line Transport. 87th.Bde. moved to ARRAS and No. 3 Coy to RACECOURSE	
	14/5/17.		Visited D.H.Q. Rain during night but fine day.	
ARRAS.	15/5/17.		Moved to ARRAS Racecourse. D.H.Q. and 86 th. Bde. to ARRAS. No. 2 Coy. and Bde. Transport moved to RACECOURSE. Fine day but colder.	
	16/5/17.		Visited H.Q. Company. Fine day.	
	17/5/17.		WANQUETIN Ammunition Dump blown up. Fine day.	
	18/5/17.		2nd./Lts. Mathews and Hulme left AUBIGNY for leave. Fine day.	
	19/5/17.		Lt. Harper arrived. 15 remounts arrived. 12 went to No.1 Coy., 1 to No 2, 1 to No.3 and 1 to No4. Heavy shelling during evening.	
	20/5/17.		Visited III Army. Very fine day.	
	21/5/17.		Inspected Hd. Qr. Company. Reconnoitered country between AGNEY and WAILLY for grazing and green forage. Wet night.	
	22/5/17.		Removed Dumps of Bdes to RACECOURSE. Very wet.	
	23/5/17.		Visited lines, rather untidy. Fine day.	

2353 Wt. W2544/1454 700,000 5/15 D. D. & L. A.D.S.S./Forms/C. 2118.

Army Form C. 2118.

WAR DIARY
or
INTELLIGENCE SUMMARY.
(Erase heading not required.)

Instructions regarding War Diaries and Intelligence Summaries are contained in F.S. Regs., Part II. and the Staff Manual respectively. Title pages will be prepared in manuscript.

Place	Date	Hour	Summary of Events and Information	Remarks and references to Appendices
ARRAS.	24/5/17.		Green forage brought in from old German line, but too young for cutting. Ammunition Dump exploded at ACHIECOURT. Dr. Casey was killed and one horse wounded. One horse evacuated. DECAUVILLE Rly. used for the first time. Fine day.	
	25/5/17.		Started Salvage by Companies. Heavy shelling. German aeroplanes came over about 7 A.M. Visited 1st. Line Transport. Very fine day.	
	26/5/17.		Enemy shelled DOULLENS Road. Companies begin to bring Salvage. Bombs in evening. Very fine.	
	27/5/17.		Shelling entrance to ARRAS. Horse Show of drivers who have had same pair of horses one year.	
	28/5/17.		Continual activity of enemy airmen. A.D.V.S. Visited Train. Draft arrives from St.Pol. Very fine day.	
	29/5/17.		Cut green forage. Dull day.	
	30/5/17.		Brought Major Labmert from Div. Depot. Saw A.A. & Q.M.G. re proposed Horse Show. Arranged duty moving of 3 and 4 Companies on account of Range. Wagon on Salvage Dump blown up and Driver wounded. Very fine day.	
	31/5/17.		C.S.M. Gibbon arrives for 89th.Fld. Ambulance. The Sports held and Div. Band played. Very fine day.	

F.W.W.
Lieut. Col. A.S.C.
Commdg. 29th. Divisional Train.

CONFIDENTAL.

WAR DIARY Of

29th. DIVISIONAL TRAIN A.S.C.

From. 1st. June, 1917   To 30th. June, 1917.

(VOLUME 16.)

Army Form C. 2118.

WAR DIARY
or
INTELLIGENCE SUMMARY.
(Erase heading not required.)

Instructions regarding War Diaries and Intelligence Summaries are contained in F.S. Regs., Part II. and the Staff Manual respectively. Title pages will be prepared in manuscript.

Place	Date	Hour	Summary of Events and Information	Remarks and references to Appendices
ARRAS.	1/6/17.		New Naval Gun bombarded district round DAINEVILLE and blew up Small Arms Dump. Visited D.H.Q. with Major Lambert, also 111 Army and met 111 Div. marching up. Very fine day.	
	2/6/17.		No.2 Coy., marched to BERNEVILLE. Interpreter Rossat went to BERNAVILLE and LUCHEUX about billets Railhead shelled. 3rd.Division arrive and taking over lines. Dull day.	
	3/6/17.		Very fine day. Left ARRAS Racecourse 7.30 a.m. No.3 Coy., shelled going to Railhead 2 men killed and 1 wounded and 3 horses killed. Arrived LUCHEUX 4 p.m.	
LUCHEUX	4/6/17.		Fine day. T.H.Q. moved to BERNAVILLE. No. 2 Coy. to EPCAMPS. 86th. Bde. First Line moved in.	
BERNAVILLE	5/6/17.		Visited 86th. 1st. Line Transport. No. 4 Coy., moved to CANAPLES with Bde Transport in that area.	
	6/6/17.		Visited 87th. and 88th. 1st.Line Transport. No.3 Coy. moved to BERNVILLERS. arranged green forage by Companies. Dr.Hill and car brought into Hd.Qrs.	
	7/6/17.		Major Lambert inspected 1st.Line Transport at CANDAS. Orders received for move of Major Lambert and Lieut. Harper to 35th. and 3rd. Divisional Trains respectively.	
	8/6/17.		Very fine day.	
	9/6/17.		Very fine day. Lt. Harper to 3rd.Div.Train. Visited Companies and 1st.Line Transport.	
	10/6/17.		Dull but fine. Major Lamberted visited Railhead. 2 Riders to St.Pol. Heavy thunder storm.	
	11/6/17.		Vet. Officer left for Bde. H.Q. Adjutant and S.S.O. went to Paris on leave. Lt.Kean took over	

Army Form C. 2118.

WAR DIARY
or
INTELLIGENCE SUMMARY.
(Erase heading not required.)

Instructions regarding War Diaries and Intelligence Summaries are contained in F. S. Regs., Part II. and the Staff Manual respectively. Title pages will be prepared in manuscript.

Place	Date	Hour	Summary of Events and Information	Remarks and references to Appendices
			Vet. duties of the Train.	
	12/6/17.		Major Lambert and Dr. Double left for 35th. Div.Train. 2nd./Lieut. Hulme acting Adjutant. Visited 1st.Line and Bde. Companies. Very fine day.	
	13/6/17.		Very fine day. Visited No.1. Company and brought back a wheeler.	
	14/6/17.		Visited 1st.Line Transport of Monmouths - not good. Visited 2 and 4 Companies. S.S.O. returned off leave to Paris.	
	15/6/17.		Very fine day. Adjutant return off leave. Saw D.H.Q. re move.	
	16/6/17.		Lovely day. Horse Show was a great success. Hd.Qr. Coy. Officers came in.	
	17/6/17.		Lieut. Challoner admitted to C.C.S. No.41. Interviewed Capt. Newton.	
	18/6/17.		Car No.239 to Workshop. Car to No.3 Coy., for Lt. Blount.to relieve Capt. Upson proceeding on leave. Monmouths, C.R.E. and 2 Field Coys.,left for north and rationed until 20th.	
	19/6/17.		Lt. Mathews struck off the strength. Visited 1st.Line Transport. Very fine day.	
	20/6/17.		Rainy day. Instructions re move. Visited 1st.Line Transport.	
	21/6/17.		Fine day. Lt. Mew transferred to No. 4 Coy. Car to No. 1 Coy. for move to GOUVES. 3 F.D. horses of No.4 Coy., evacuated.	
	22/6/17.		Went to D.H.Q re move. Advance party left from CANDAS 7.30 a.m. 2nd/Lieut. Garle arrives and	

Army Form C. 2118.

WAR DIARY
or
INTELLIGENCE SUMMARY.
(Erase heading not required.)

Instructions regarding War Diaries and Intelligence Summaries are contained in F.S. Regs., Part II. and the Staff Manual respectively. Title pages will be prepared in manuscript.

Place	Date	Hour	Summary of Events and Information	Remarks and references to Appendices
	23/6/17.		is posted to No. 3 Coy. Visited 1st.Line Transport.	
	24/6/17.		Fine day. No.1 Coy., arrive at GOUVES. Instructions re move issued to Companies. Fine day. Remounts arrive. Visited Coys. O.C. and S.S.O. of 20th.Division arrive. New time table re move.	
	25th/6/17.		Mons. Rossat proceeded to PROVEN re billets. Order for move on 26th. received. Rainy day.	
	26/6/17.		Moved to PROVEN by car. Saw H.Q.D.T. and No.3 Coy. detrain. Arranged for Nos.2 and 4 Covs. to remain at PROVEN. No. 3 Coy., moved to forward area. Fine day.	
PROVEN	27/6/17.		No. 2 and 4 Coys. arrive at PROVEN. Capt. Newton went C.C.S. without leave and was detained.	
	28/6/17.		Very dull day. Visited sites at INTERNATIONAL CORNER. Visited D.H.Q. twice during day. Railhead, PROVEN. Lt. Challoner back to duty. Dr. Hill and Car to No.1 Coy. for move.	
	29/6/17.		2 Wheelers to XIV Corps to make packsaddlery at S.25.b.7.6. Railhead PROVEN. Capt. Newton took over command of No. 4 Coy., from Lt. Macmanaway. Certificate sent to D.H.Q. Shelling area at night. Moved to INTERNATIONAL CORNER.	
INTERNAT- IONAL CORNER.	30/6/17.		Went to INTERNATIONAL CORNER Railhead at 11 a.m. No. 4 Coy. contravened orders and went to Railhead before time×~~Capt. Newton~~ Lt. Blount transferred to No. 1 Cov. Shelling area at night. S.S.O's Car to Workshops. Wet day.	

Lieut. Col. A.S.C.
Commanding 29th.Divisional Train.

CONFIDENTIAL.

WAR DIARY of

29th. DIVISIONAL TRAIN, A. S. C.

From, 1st. July, 1917.   To. 31st. July, 1917.

(VOLUME 17.)

H.Q.,
29TH DIVL. TRAIN.
No.....................
Date....................

Army Form C. 2118.

WAR DIARY
or
INTELLIGENCE SUMMARY.
(Erase heading not required.)

Instructions regarding War Diaries and Intelligence Summaries are contained in F. S. Regs., Part II. and the Staff Manual respectively. Title pages will be prepared in manuscript.

Place	Date	Hour	Summary of Events and Information	Remarks and references to Appendices
INTERNAT-IONAL CORNER	1/7/17.		Went to Railhead. 10 Tons of Coal removed from WIPPEHOEK. Visited 1st.Line and D.H.Q.	
	2/7/17.		Aircraft very busy. Reported to D.H.Q. and unmanageable horse in 3 Coy. Sent pass book home. Visited 1st. Line Transport. Very fine day.	
	3/7/17		Heavy shelling of back area all night. S.S.O. went to DUNKIRK in Damler. Mange in No.4 Coy. Visited 1st. Line Transport.	
	4/7/17.		Aircraft busy. Shelling during night. Report re mange sent to D.H.Q. Saw Horse Expert XIV Corps Visited Coys. Hot and close also rain during the night.	
	5/7/17.		Shelling back areas in early morning. Difficulty re coal. Railhead late. Visit Railhead. Orders re Kings Visit.	
	6/7/17.		G.O.C. Division inspected Train Head Quarters and No. 3 Coy. Gave orders to entrench. Wrote re shortage of horses. Gas Alarm at night. Enemy Planes Planes passed over, dropping bombs. O.C. 55th. Divisional Train called. Car back from Workshops. Fine day.	
	7/7/17.		Visited Coys and inspected horses. No. 4 Coy dipped, suspected mange animals. Heavy shelling all round Camp. Received Table re Advanced Transport of advance. Gas alarm at night. in case	
	8/7/17		Very wet. Visited Headquarter Coy and found them in Good order at HOUTKERKK:also 39th. Train Headquarters. Day quiet. 3 Reinforcements arrived.	

Army Form C. 2118.

WAR DIARY
or
INTELLIGENCE SUMMARY.
(Erase heading not required.)

Instructions regarding War Diaries and Intelligence Summaries are contained in F.S. Regs., Part II. and the Staff Manual respectively. Title pages will be prepared in manuscript.

Place	Date	Hour	Summary of Events and Information	Remarks and references to Appendices
	9/7/17.		Visited 39th.Divisional Train. Advance Dump Supplies unable to arrive owing to the line being blown up. Leave allotment large. Dull day.	
	10/7/17.		Heavy shelling all day. Baggage waggons being used for R.E. work and Camouflage work. Yukon Packs sent in for altering. A.S.C. Officers under Medically examined. 30	
	11/7/17.		Car out of Order - Seige Park Repaired it. Secret letter re gas attack received. 20 Tons of coal drawn. Lieut. Challoner to C.C.S. Very fine day.	
	12/7/17.		Fine day. Brigades moved round.	
	13/7/17.		Hills car sent to Workshops. No. 3 Coy. settled camp. No.4 Coy settled camp, difficult owing to shortage of horses. Fine day.	
	14/7/17.		Dull day and rain during night. Visited Coys. Sent Belgian Interpreters re Billets.	
	15/7/17.		Coys changed camps. Yukon Packs to again be altered. Visited No. 1 Coy. Rain and unsettled.	
	16/7/17.		Sent Adjutant to fix up Transport for Artillery to be attached to 38th. Divisional Troops. Rossat, the Interpreter, left for V Corps. Wheelers very slow on Yukon Packs. Fine Day.	
	17/7/17.		Coal train came in and No. 3 Coy started unloading. N.C.O. Artificers troublesome in 3.Coy. Speeding up alterations in Yukon Packs. Fine day. Large Leave Allotment of 9th.inst. cancelled.	
	18/7/17.		Camp shelled about 7 am. Sgt. Powell killed and 7 men wounded(one very badly) 5 horses wounded	

Army Form C. 2118.

WAR DIARY
or
INTELLIGENCE SUMMARY.
(Erase heading not required.)

Instructions regarding War Diaries and Intelligence Summaries are contained in F.S. Regs., Part II. and the Staff Manual respectively. Title pages will be prepared in manuscript.

Place	Date	Hour	Summary of Events and Information	Remarks and references to Appendices
PROVEN	19/7/17.		1 had to be shot. These were all attached from 20th. Div. Train. 1 of 2 Coys. wagons destroyed by a shell. Captain Taylor went to find a new camp for No. 2 Coy. 34th. D.S.C. objected to lorry being used for Postal Services for Divl. Troops. Enemy started shelling vicinity of camp about 11 pm. Dull and rainy.	
	20/7/17.		T.H.Q. and No 2 Coy moved to back area. Sent letter to D.D.S. & T. re system of refilling and drawing from Railhead. Mistake over coal Train - S.S.O. contradictory wire. Rain but afterwards fine.	
			Sent Adjutant off in car to put coal train straight. Arranged temporary transfer of W.O. of No. 1 Coy to No.4 and vice versa, hope transfer will improve No. 4 Coy. No. 4 Coy written to about not having sign boards up. Saw Supply Officer No. 2 Coy about complaints of shortage of forage. Fine day.	
	21/7/17.		D.H.Q. arrived at PROVEN. Saw D.D.S. & T. who went round Train Coys. Saw "Q" Staff. Dull but dry.	
	22/7/17.		Very fine day. Visited D.H.Q. Railhead delayed 45 minutes.	
	23/7/17		Fine day. Visited Coys.	
	24/7/17.		Yukon Packs hastened. No.2 and No 4 Coys changed over. Divl Order re slackness of N.C.Os and	

Army Form C. 2118.

WAR DIARY
or
INTELLIGENCE SUMMARY.
(Erase heading not required.)

Instructions regarding War Diaries and Intelligence Summaries are contained in F. S. Regs., Part II. and the Staff Manual respectively. Title pages will be prepared in manuscript.

Place	Date	Hour	Summary of Events and Information	Remarks and references to Appendices
	25/7/17.		Men turning out in streets. Vegetables purchased from DUNKIRK. Fine day.	
	26/7/17.		Yukon Packs finally delived and receipts obtained. Complaint re No. 2 Coy leaving Paters Camp dirty. No. 4 Coy left camp dirty-, took O.C. Coy to look at it. Corps Historical Notes called for. Horses from Calais arrive; but very poor class. Went to D.H.Q 20th. Division. 50 Tons of coal unloaded. Raining.	
	27/7/17.		3 Officers given leave. 65 Tons of Coal arrive International Corner. Heavy Artillery fire all afternoon. 50 Prisoners came in. Fine day.	
	28/7/17.		Went to No. 1 Coy. News of Divl. Artillery moving: O.C. No. 1 Coy and S.O. came in re move. Extra Artillery attached to No. 2 coy for feeding. Fine day.	
	29/7/17		Visited Coys. Dull day.	
	30/7/17		Visited D.H.Q. and Coys. Order received re entering Railhead by South and leaving by North. Dull went to OLHAIN. Orders received for 3 Coy. to move up with Brigade.	
	31/7/17		Offencive started, preceeded by very heavy bombardment and barrage .Objectives gained. 3 Coy. moved to Forest Camp, bad ground and little or no cover for men. Heavy bombardment at dusk.Enemy shelling back areas. Raining.	

Lieut. Colonel, A.S.C.
Commanding 29th.Divisional Train.

H.Q.,
29TH DIVL. TRAIN.

No..........
Date..........

Vol 18

C O N F I D E N T I A L

W A R D I A R Y of the

29th D I V I S I O N A L T R A I N.

Army Service Corps.

From 1st August 1917 to 31st August 1917.

Volume 18.

WAR DIARY
or
INTELLIGENCE SUMMARY

Army Form C. 2118.

Place	Date	Hour	Summary of Events and Information	Remarks and references to Appendices
PROVEN	1-8-17		Visited Railhead, congestion owing to park train arriving late.	
"	2-8-17		Went D.H.Q re move. 2 H.D Horses of 4 Co evacuated, eye trouble	
"	3-8-17		Major Wright took over command of M Train from Lieut Col Syms. My Syms to H Reserve Park 6 H D, 9 L D Horses arrived at Railhead, distributed to companies	
"	4-8-17		Visited the Brigade Companies & inspected lines. Lieut E&G Provost struck off strength of Train, on transfer to the Infantry	
"	5-8-17		Had a conference of Co Commanders at H.Q. Visited Guards Div Train in connection with relief.	
"	6-8-17		No 9 & 18 Companies moved to new area, on the Division moving up into the line. Sent Mr Marreau returned from leave. 2 H T Drivers joined from the Base on reinforcements.	
"	7-8-17		K.H Company move to new area. All companies draw by Horse Transport from INTERNATIONAL CORNER, Refilling point on the main road, 1 mile South of ELVERDINGHE. Visited Head Quarter Company of the Train at 20/S3/c 7.5. 1 Heavy Draught evacuated sick, shown remount	
Post 20 S/21.C 3.6	8-8-17		Train Head Quarters moved, SSO Office withdrawn from Divisional Head Quarters to Train Head Quarters. All Infantry Brigades going into the line are furnished with 3 days supplies over and above current days issue. Imperial Company wagons at Railhead	continued

Army Form C. 2118.

WAR DIARY
or
INTELLIGENCE SUMMARY.
(Erase heading not required.)

Instructions regarding War Diaries and Intelligence Summaries are contained in F. S. Regs., Part II. and the Staff Manual respectively. Title pages will be prepared in manuscript.

Place	Date	Hour	Summary of Events and Information	Remarks and references to Appendices
SHEET 20				
5/27 & 3 5	8-8-17		Visited Nº 2 3 + 6º Lines and inspected their horses. Corporal Drake transferred from 182 to Head Quarter Cavalry Corps for duty	
"	9.6.17		1000 Point Time at ONDANK DUMP field unit units for rending all the fixing lines. Inspected 1st Line Transport of the Middlesex Regt and Lancashire Fusiliers. Visited Railhead new site for Head Quarters 69 at 20/S 16 & 75.	
"	10.6.17		Great delay at INTERNATIONAL CORNER Railhead owing to the road material which was dumped overnight not being cleared from the yard. Section 26 of 2 Park Farm for the 2d Division was left 100 yards outside the yard so that nearly all the supplies had to be man handled to the wagons. Got D.A.D.S. 5th Army to come out and see the condition of things and made a written report. D.A.D.V.S. inspected the 3 Brigade Companies horses. Inspected Head Quarter Company's new lines very good standing. Issued 1500 Petrol tins at ONDANK unit watch. Inspected 1st Line Transport of Royal Fusiliers and Duke Fusiliers. Great improvement at Railhead and the road material had been removed. Issued an extra wagon to the 68th Brigade. Pte Evans appointed Corporal (paid) and transferred to 66 Divisional Supply Column. Captain Upton returned from leave.	
"	11.6.17			

WAR DIARY
or
INTELLIGENCE SUMMARY.
(Erase heading not required.)

Army Form C. 2118.

Place	Date	Hour	Summary of Events and Information	Remarks and references to Appendices
Sheet 20 S/27c.3.5	12.8.17		1 Driver admitted to hospital in England from leave (3.6.9)	
"	13.8.17		Captain H.K. Wallace RAMC transferred to 87 Brigade Field Ambulance on reduction of establishment. Wrote O.C. Records re insufficient NCO's. Had experiments to find suitable type of "Tommy Cooker" inspected. No.2 3i/h Companies lines, cookhouses & Permanent latrines have been erected by companies. 1 NCO reported at Divisional Gas School for a course of instruction.	
"	14.8.17		Visited Head Quarter Company lines, camp bivouacs etc. Received an order to keep 4, 50 gallon tanks at GREEN MILL (1500 yards East of BOESINGHE) continuously supplied with water, until battle is over. Visited GREEN MILL with Field Maur who was detailed for this duty together with Adjutant & SSO, who inspected ration dumps at PILLS DUMP. 1 Sergeant (Sani) evacuated with Wrote opinion re withdrawing 1 NCO from No.168 to take charge of transport unit Army Brigades RFA. 1 HD Horse reamer from Remounts posted to 169.	
"	16.8.17		Lieut T. Devine joined from the Base and posted to No.168. Each Infantry Brigade drew an extra charger sufficient before going into the line and under drew one day on coming out. Inspected 86 Brigade 15 line transport. Captain J. Brown proceeded on leave. Lieut W.E. Wickham temporarily transferred to 368. Sent SSO's Motor Car to the workshops for overhauling	

WAR DIARY
or
INTELLIGENCE SUMMARY

(Erase heading not required.)

Army Form C. 2118.

Place	Date	Hour	Summary of Events and Information	Remarks and references to Appendices
Sheet 20				
S/21 c.3	5/17 5.17		2nd RTR the many attempts to tempt to the Mechanical Transport Branch of the Corps, allotment of gear of us to the end of this month, 1 Blandt (Brun) evacuated to Base unexpected reported the arrival of unarmed latrine by Bombardier to Divisional Head Quarters. 1 Runner and 1 Horse Head Quarter badly burned and evacuated. Instruction received to reduce Strength of the strength of	
			The Same as 11-6-17	
"	16.6.17		Inspected the Head Quarters Company on parade "dismounted". The 2nd Guards Brigade (3515 Men S.H.D. 3562 D. Horses) attached to the Division for inspection.	
"	18.6.17		Temporarily transferred 2 NCO's to take temporary of a platoon on the efficiency of Inexperienced 2nd Lt AB Neal joined from the Base for duty posted to No 369 applied to OC OSB for cadre for removal to garrison of SStray Nelson & Corp lt. Furlan both unfit for their positions had sent these NCO's beyond me as the part of the autumn from taking	
"	20.6.17		Captain D'Tzants proceeded on leave. Captain Aytoun, Essex Regiment attached for instruction. Inspected 1 Sqdn Transport of Machine Gun Companies. Commenced "Classes of Instruction" for Sergeants and Corporals under RSM Staff Sergeant Major JO Gould. Point out to these NCO's their lack of knowledge of their duties and want of pride in their positions they were cautioned that if, after further instruction they could not prove themselves	Cavalry

2353 Wt. W2544/1454 700,000 5/15 D. D. & L. A.D.S.S./Forms/C. 2118.

WAR DIARY or INTELLIGENCE SUMMARY

Army Form C. 2118.

Place	Date	Hour	Summary of Events and Information	Remarks and references to Appendices
Sheet 2-C	Rendinghem			
	5/29 c.3 5/30.8.17		Thompson.	
	31-8-17		1st for whom positions they would be reviewed for inefficiency. 3 Drivers transferred to HQ Mechanical Transport Depot CALAIS. Horse Transport & Mechanical Transport visited Staff Captain 88 Brigade to inform method of making Tommys cookers. Selected waiting point for the Brigade in the forward area, close to the transport lines at MICHEL FARM.	
	1-6-17		88 Brigade arrived at MICHEL FARM. Went to WATOU, inspected free forage green forage being obtained. Made arrangements regarding the amount to be cut daily and for providing necessary transport. Visited Head Quarters 88th during shelling. 1 Esmin Corporal (80) evacuated, sick, also 1 Horse Transport Driver 1 HD Horse evacuated (1.88.)	
	2-6-17		Order received to move back on the 5th to PROVEN area, each Brigade Company R.MC Brigade area. Applied and received 535 Francs grant from Divisional Ration Depôt for the Train, 1 Mule (366) evacuated.	
	3-6-17		Divided into Quarter Guards Divisional Train in reference to the move, and inspected camps to be handed over by Companies. Rendezvous of H T Drivers fit for general Service to Head Quarters 1 HD Horse (468) evacuated.	
	4-6-17		1 H D Horse (660) evacuated. Rendered report on 1st Line Transport of 86-87 & 88th Brigade to	Continued

Army Form C. 2118.

WAR DIARY
or
INTELLIGENCE SUMMARY.
(Erase heading not required.)

Instructions regarding War Diaries and Intelligence Summaries are contained in F. S. Regs. Part II. and the Staff Manual respectively. Title pages will be prepared in manuscript.

Place	Date	Hour	Summary of Events and Information	Remarks and references to Appendices
Sheet 20	Continued			
S/7.c.3.5.	3.6.17		Divisional Head Quarters. Went to see a horse purposely taken as jibber No 14 B.S. and considered it was no use, replied to D.D.Remounts 5th Army for instructions for evacuation orders. Infantry Brigades now at PROVEN AREA companies taking over Grenade Divisional Train Camps as follows - 5 B⁴ Sheet 19/W 30.a.7.5, 3 B⁴ 27/E.4.a.7.5, 4 B⁴ 27/F
"	4.3.17		2.a.6.2. 14th Div. Artillery administered by Guards Divisional Train did O.S.P. Paget-Cooke proceeded on leave. Capt J.S.Crome returned from leave. Captain D.Granton called for permission to apply for extension of leave. Received instructions in alteration of Sheet No 1st Army Vet Laura allotment to September Siracourt (64) via Boulogne. All leave suspended for the day. N⁰ 2 & 6 B⁴ drew from PROVEN. N⁰ 1 & drew by Horse Transport from INTERNATIONAL CORNER, the artillery remaining on the line N⁰ 3 B⁴ drew by Mechanical Transport from PROVEN.
"	5.6.17		From Head Quarters move to Sheet 27/E.12.d.6.6. Wet unsatisfactory. Called in at D.D.S/T 5th Army with regard to the supply of stores for baths forage. Requirements will be sent up on the Pack Team daily from 7th September inclusive. Bread is now distilled to Divisions by Corps instead of D.S/T. 3 days supply only to be held by Divisions. 15 Brigade R.H.A. & 14 Brigade R.F.A. ordered to move into rest areas.
SHEET 27 E/12.d.6.6	20.6.17		

2353 Wt. W2514/1454 700,000 5/15 D. D. & L. A.D.S.S./Forms/C. 2118.

WAR DIARY or INTELLIGENCE SUMMARY

Army Form C. 2118.

Place	Date	Hour	Summary of Events and Information	Remarks and references to Appendices
Ref 29	continued		area	
E/12 d 6 6.80 1/7			near CALAIS. Leave suspended on day. Major B. Gillam proceeded on leave. S.n.l. 1 S Sgt. Farrier le Vilunary leave for Course of Instruction at CALAIS. 1 french Interpreter (ANDRE) Accompanied the CRA finally.	
"	31-8-17		Visited Head Quarters 29' Divisional Artillery and Head Quarter Companies or more. I arranged for detachment of supply and baggage wagons of Head Quarter Coys (H.Q.III) Divisional Ammunition Column & Trench Mortar Battery which is to remain in their present locations, to carry to their present camp and draw supplies from Guards Divisional M.T. of Head Quarter Company actually arranges supplies for Hampstead HQr from 15 Sept. DCS Union.	

S. Wright
Lieut Colonel A.S.C.
Comdg 29th Divisional Train

29th DIVISIONAL TRAIN.

WAR DIARY.

SEPTEMBER 1917.

In the Field
2-10-17,

H.Q.,
29TH DIVL. TRAIN.

No.
Date.

Army Form C. 2118.

WAR DIARY
or
INTELLIGENCE SUMMARY.
(Erase heading not required.)

Instructions regarding War Diaries and Intelligence Summaries are contained in F.S. Regs., Part II. and the Staff Manual respectively. Title pages will be prepared in manuscript.

Place	Date	Hour	Summary of Events and Information	Remarks and references to Appendices
PROVEN	1/9/17.		Headquarter Coy with Baggage and Supply wagons of 15th. Bde.R.H.A. and 17th. Bde.R.F.A. move to WORMHOUDT en route for POLINCOVE. Supplies for consumption 3rd.inst. delivered by M.T. to Refilling point in new area. Inspected 1st.Line Transport of Worters and Essex Regt., and also No. 4 Company of Train. Inspected clothing of this Coy. which requires to be improved and mens quarters put up. No green vegetables or extra forage received. 'Phoned up D.D.S.&T.R regarding these supplies. Received notice that 48 General Duty men would be relieved by other than category "A" men. No. 1 Company evacuate 1 H.D. horse. Dull day.	
"	2/9/17.		Inspected 1st.Line Transport of N.F.L.D and Hants Regts. No green vegetables or extra forage at Railhead. 4 Tons cabbage purchased locally and issued to Units. Attended Railhead. Supplies for Artillery delivered by M.T. to POLINCOVE. Sent Adjt. to see H.Q. Coy. in new area. No.2 Company evacuate 3 H.D. Horses.	
"	3/9/17.		1 G.S. Wagon drawn to complete No.1 Coy. Accompanied Brig'. Comm'd. 86th.Bde. on his inspection of 1st.Line Transport. Attended conference on Winter arrangements at Divl. H.Q. The Adjutant went on leave.	
"	4/9/17.		Attended Railhead and visited 86th.Bde. Refilling Point. 5 lorries from Guards D.S.C. will be and 5 from 38th.D.S.C. will be detailed daily from to-morrow to deliver rations to 5th. add	

2353 W. W2344/1451 700,000 5/15 D.D.&L. A.D.S.S./Forms/C. 2118.

Army Form C. 2118.

WAR DIARY
or
INTELLIGENCE SUMMARY.
(Erase heading not required.)

Instructions regarding War Diaries and Intelligence Summaries are contained in F.S. Regs., Part II. and the Staff Manual respectively. Title pages will be prepared in manuscript.

Place	Date	Hour	Summary of Events and Information	Remarks and references to Appendices
			and 76th.Army Bdes. R.F.A., which are being administered by us. Drew extra hay at Railhead at 4 Tons per day from 1st. inclusive. Packtrain contained 4 oz. potatoe ration; also 2000 rations short which makes the percentage xxickxxxxxxxx of bread and meat low. 3 H.D. Horses arrive and posted to 4 Coy. Arrangements for lorries to help 3 and 4 Coys drawing. Reverted=Tucker and C/Watson, sent former to Base and transferred latter to No.2 Coy.	
"	5/9/17.		Attended Railhead. ½ ration of Fresh vegetable only. 3 Tons potatoes purchased. Visited No.4 Coy's lines. Visited No.1 Coy at RUMINGHEM. A/S.S.M. Ashton (No.100v.) reverted to permanent Rank of Sgt. for "Inefficiency" and dispatched to Base. Classification of General Duty men called for. Fine Day.	
"	6/9/17.		Middlesex and Royal Fusiliers move into forward area for work under C.E. XIV Corps, and will be administered by 20th.Divl. Train, from Railhead drawing on 7th.inst. Supply wagons attached to 20th.Divl.Train. Conference of Company Commanders, and pointed out their duty of instructing their Officers and N.C.Os. more highly. Extra Artillery grouped to 87th.Group. Wet day.	
"	7/9/17.		Dull day. Notification of Major Holman posted. 2/Lt.Forbes arrived and posted to 2 Coy. 1 Dr. Whr. of No. 3 Company sent to Base "Surplus to Establishment."	
"	8/9/17.		15th.Bde.R.H.A. and 17th.Bde.R.F.A. with H.Q. Coy. ordered to move from POLINCOVE to WORMHOUDT on	

Army Form C. 2118.

WAR DIARY
or
INTELLIGENCE SUMMARY.
(Erase heading not required.)

Instructions regarding War Diaries and Intelligence Summaries are contained in F. S. Regs., Part II. and the Staff Manual respectively. Title pages will be prepared in manuscript.

Place	Date	Hour	Summary of Events and Information	Remarks and references to Appendices
"	9/9/17.		on 10th.inst.,to old positions near ONDANK on 11th.inst.	
"	10/9/17.		Move of Artillery and H.Q. Coy. cancelled at 10-30 p.m. No.2 Company evacuate 1 H.D. to M.V.S. 1 Batty. 17th. Bde.R.F.A. armxHxxxCxyx marched from POLINCOVE to HERZEELE Area. Bread & Meat for Artillery and H.Q. Coy. drawn from PROVEN and delivered by lorry to POLINCOVE Area.Remainder of rations and forage drawn from WATTEN by H.T. 1 H.T. Driver from Base posted to 3 Coy. Capt. Franks from leave. Fine day.	
"	11/9/17.		Bread and Meat for Artillery and H.Q. Coy. drawn from INTERNATIONAL CORNER and delivered by lorry to POLINCOVE Area. Remainder of supplies drawn from WATTEN by H.T. Capt.Franks reported to Act as S.S.O. No. 3 Company evacuate 1 H.T. Dr to the Base by No.3 Coy. Farr. S.Sgt.Duncan (2 Coy.) returned from Vet Class at CALAIS. Batty of 17th. Bde. R.F.A.moved from HERZEELE to	
"	12/9/17.		forward area and being administered by 36th.Divl. XXXXX Artillery. The 76th.Army Bde. R.F.A. administered by 20th. Divl. Artillery, to-day.	
"	12/9/17.		Major Holman arrived . No. 1 Company commenced move, via WORMHOUDT and left 2 H.D. and 1 Rider at "Mairie" there. Fine Day.	
"	13/9/17.		Arrangements re Divl. Artillery move. 1. L.D. Brse from 5th.Army Bde. R.F.A. to 4 Company. Fine.	
"	14/9/17.		Fine day. Sgt. Bland from Guards Divl. Train for C.S.M. No. 4 Coy. 1 L.D. from z Batty. R.H.A.	

Army Form C.2118.

WAR DIARY
or
INTELLIGENCE SUMMARY.
(Erase heading not required.)

Instructions regarding War Diaries and Intelligence Summaries are contained in F. S. Regs., Part II. and the Staff Manual respectively. Title pages will be prepared in manuscript.

Place	Date	Hour	Summary of Events and Information	Remarks and references to Appendices
"	15/9/17.		Fine Day. 1 Dr. Sadd. of No.1 Coy evacuated to Base sick. Sgt.Rogulski, No.4 Coy. evacuated to Base sick.	
"	16/9/17.		Fine day. Capt. Newton from Leave. 1 Dr. No.4 Coy. evacuated to Base, sick.	
"	17/9/17.		No.1 Company evacuate 1 H.D. Horse. Sent War Diaries to Records. 1Dr. Farr. and 1 Dr. Whr. from Base, former to No.1 Coy and the latter to No. 4 Coy.	
"	18/9/17.		Fine day. 1 Dr.(No. 3 Coy) reported as absent off leave and now found to be in Hospital in London. 1 H.D. evacuated to M.V.S. by No.1 Company.	
"	19/9/17.		C.S.M.Mole reported and posted to No. 4 Coy.as S.S.Major,(from 21st.D.S.C.) S.S.M. Anderton to return to No.1 Coy. also exchange of batmen and horses, vice Ashton. 2/Lt. Balmer reported and posted to No. 4 Company.	
S/27 c 8-5	20/9/17.		Fine Day. Train Headquarters moved to S/27.c.8.5. vice Guards Divl Train H.Q. The Bde. Coys also move to the following locations :- No.2 Coy.,28/A.3.d.5.7., No.3 Coy.,20/S/27.c.3.5. and No.4 Coy.,28/A.8.2.8.3. Railhead International Corner. "Tommy's Cookers are being made from dripping and paraffin by Supply Officers - and are issued under instructions of S.S.O.. The 88th. Bde. are in the Line. Refilling Point for 86th.Bde.ELVERDINGHE. The 86th.,87th. and 88th. Bdes. Refilling Point is EIKHOEK.	

Army Form C. 2118.

WAR DIARY
or
INTELLIGENCE SUMMARY.
(Erase heading not required.)

Instructions regarding War Diaries and Intelligence Summaries are contained in F. S. Regs., Part II. and the Staff Manual respectively. Title pages will be prepared in manuscript.

Place	Date	Hour	Summary of Events and Information	Remarks and references to Appendices
S/29c.3.5	21/9/17.		Fine Day. 1 H.T. Dr. from Base and posted to No.3 Coy. D.H.Q. still at PROVEN.	
"	22/9/17.		D.H.Q. move to "J" Camp.	
"	23/9/17.		Fine day. Capt. Upson on leave to PARIS.	
"	24/9/17.		Fine day. Lt.Blount at T.H.Q. re taking over new camp near INTERNATIONAL CORNER. Exchanged Cpl.Sargeant and Pritchard Scott and Schofield, for disciplinary reasons. Adjutant commenced classes of instruction for Subalterns, Mondays, Wednesday, and Friday. Inspected 1st.Line Transport of 87th.Inft. Bde.	
"	25/9/17.		10 H.D. Horses arrive PROVEN. 6 to No.1 Coy. and 4 to No.2 Coy. Cant, Viveashe goes on leave. Inspected 1st.Line Transport of 86th.Bde. Lieut. Paget-Cooke transferred to England for Infantry. Sgt. Sandiford from 4 to 3 Coy. to adjust strength. Hill comes from shops and VAUXHALL Car	
"	26/9/17.		Fineday. Lt. Mew goes on leave. Order to Coys to commence erecting huts and lines, etc., for Winter. "Daimler" to Shops. 2/Lt.Forbes to 4 Coy. temporary duty as S.O. No 1 Coy evacuate 1 Dr. sick; also 1 H.D. Horse. Capt. Upson returned off leave to Paris.	
"	27/9/17.		Fine day. Communication re R. Dublin Fusiliers and Guernsey Light XXX Infantry, change of 1st. Line Transport etc. No.1 Coy. moved to 28/A.8.d.0.4. Bombs dropped on Railhead and near Train Headquarters at 11 p.m.	

Army Form C. 2118.

WAR DIARY
or
INTELLIGENCE SUMMARY.
(Erase heading not required.)

Instructions regarding War Diaries and Intelligence Summaries are contained in F. S. Regs., Part II. and the Staff Manual respectively. Title pages will be prepared in manuscript.

Place	Date	Hour	Summary of Events and Information	Remarks and references to Appendices
DO S/21 c.3.5	28/9/17.		No.1 Coy. evacuate 1 Dr. to Base, sick. 1 Dr. Whr., No.4 Coy. sent to 48th.Division, Surplus to Establishment. Fine day.	
"	29/9/17.		Fine day. Sent report on 1st.Line Transport of 86th. and 87th. Bdes., also requirement note to D.A.D.O.S. Leave allotment for October, 76.	
"	30/9/17.		Fine day. No. 4 Company move. Guards Divisional Artillery return from rest, and will draw from R.H. with 29ᵗʰ Divⁿ from Octr. 1ᵗ.	

S. Wright
Lieut.Colonel, A.S.C.,
Comdg., 29th.Divisional Train.

29th. DIVISIONAL TRAIN.

WAR DIARY

for

OCTOBER, 1917.

Volume 21

Army Form C. 2118.

WAR DIARY
or
INTELLIGENCE SUMMARY.
(Erase heading not required.)

Instructions regarding War Diaries and Intelligence Summaries are contained in F. S. Regs., Part II. and the Staff Manual respectively. Title pages will be prepared in manuscript.

Place	Date	Hour	Summary of Events and Information	Remarks and references to Appendices
International Corner	1/10/17.		2 I.D. and 2 H.D. of Headquarters Company destroyed by shell fire. Railhead, International Corner. Guards Divisional Artillery taken over from Guards Division.	
	2/10/17.		89th Army Brigade R.F.A. attached. Their Transport found to be in very bad condition. Deficiencies in personnel and animals made up, and report sent to Divisional Headquarters.	
	3/10/17.		Nos. 2 and 3 Coys at BARNES and BAGGALLAY Farms respectively carrying on with stabling and huts for winter. Still undecided as to whether No.4 Company is to move from EIKHOEK. Advice received that Guards Divisional Train will take over our Camps on the 5th. Inspected PATERS Farm with a view to putting Train Coys in when Guards move up. Very poor accommodation there and no shelter for horses.	
	4/10/17.		Instructions received from Division to attach Captain C.E.Browne to "Q" Branch for instruction. 2/Lieut. Hulme from No.2 Company to Train H.Q. as Acting Adjutant.	
	5/10/17.		Guards Divisional Train move into BAGGALLAY and BARNES Farms, Nos. 2 & 3 Companies moving to PATERS Farm, and fields adjacent. No. 4 Company remain at EIKHOEK. Refilling Point for Brigade Groups at PATERS FARM.	
	6/10/17.		3rd. Guards Brigade attached from Guards Division.	
	7/10/17.		Guards Divisional Artillery and 3rd. Guards Brigade taken over by Guards Brigade.	

Army Form C. 2118.

WAR DIARY
or
INTELLIGENCE SUMMARY.
(Erase heading not required.)

Instructions regarding War Diaries and Intelligence Summaries are contained in F. S. Regs., Part II. and the Staff Manual respectively. Title pages will be prepared in manuscript.

Place	Date	Hour	Summary of Events and Information	Remarks and references to Appendices
	8/10/17.		57th.Divisional Artillery administered by 29th.Division. Orders received to take over from 17th.Divisional Train in PROVEN AREA. Visited 17th. Divisional Train Headquarters and arranged to take over PARDOE Camp for No.2 Company and Train Headquarters and PASTURE Camp for No. 3 Company. No. 4 Company to the Corps Staging Area.	
	9/10/17.		Dull day. Dr. Wiggs at 1 L.D., No, 4 Company wounded. Lieut. Horris from Base and posted to No. 4 Company. 1/Corporal and 3 Private Clerks from Base and posted to Companies	
	10/10/17.		Train Headquarters, No.2,3 and 4 Companies move to PROVEN Area. Railhead for Brigades at PROVEN. 52nd. Infantry Brigade and 47th.D.S.C. taken over from 17th.Division. Pack Trains exchanged by mutual arrangement with 17th.Division owing to there having been insufficient time to notify alteration of Railhead. Headquarters Company remain at INTERNATIONAL CORNER 29th.Divisional Artillery and 57th.Divisional Artillery handed over to 17th.Division. 5th.Army Brigade F.F.A. attached to Headquarters Company for feeding.	
PROVEN.	11/10/17.		A/Sgt.Frith proceeded to England for course of instruction prior to a Commission in the Corps.	
	12/10/17.		Captain Taylor proceeded on leave. Cpl. Salem tried by F.G.C.M. Rain.	
	13/10/17.		Wet day. Maps of 5th.Army Area,Routine Orders and Gas Orders returned to D.H.Q. 50 Tons of coal cleared. Advance party for new Area despatched.	

Army Form C. 2118.

WAR DIARY
or
INTELLIGENCE SUMMARY.
(Erase heading not required.)

Instructions regarding War Diaries and Intelligence Summaries are contained in F.S. Regs., Part II. and the Staff Manual respectively. Title pages will be prepared in manuscript.

Place	Date	Hour	Summary of Events and Information	Remarks and references to Appendices
	14/10/17.		Instructions for move to 3rd.Army received. No.T4/108268 A/Cpl. McLennon reverted to Driver for drunkeness. T/32008 Cpl. Salem reduced to Driver by F.G.C.M. for "Absence when returning off leave".	
	15/10/17.		No.3 Company entrained for Third Army Area. D.D.S.& T. visited Train Headquarters and inspected No. 2 Company's lines. 1 H.D. horse evacuated to Guards Mobile Vet. Section.	
	16/10/17.		Train Headquarters and No.2 Company and No. 4 Company entrain for Third Army Area. 2 Bdes. draw supplies from PROVEN. 1 Bde. draw supplies from BEAUMETZ. Headquarters Company with 29th. Divisional Artillery remain in ELVEDINGHE Area and draw from International Corner.	
BASSEUX	17/10/17.		Train H.Q. at BASSEUX. No. 2 Company at HENDECOURT. No.3 Company at BAILLEUIVAL. No. 4 Company BIEUVILLERS. Railhead BOISLEUX.	
HENDECOURT	18/10/17.		Train H.Q. move to HENDECOURT. 1 Wagon (No.1Coy.) destroyed by Shell fire. 2/Lieut. Wells goes on leave. Cpl. Whitbourne,No.3 Coy.,appointed Sergeant. Pte. Sands,No.1 Company,appointed to Corporal an transferred to No. 2 Company.	
	19/10/17.		Straw for Huts urgently required. Coal to all th Baths. Drew 5 extra tents for accomodation. 1 Cpl. (Issuer) No.3 Coy.,evacuated. 3 Dr. From Base to Companies.	
	20/10/17.		Straw obtained off Rail and spoiled hay for billetting from "F" Corps Supply Column . 1 Rider,	

Army Form C. 2118.

WAR DIARY
or
INTELLIGENCE SUMMARY.
(Erase heading not required.)

Instructions regarding War Diaries and Intelligence Summaries are contained in F. S. Regs. Part II. and the Staff Manual respectively. Title pages will be prepared in manuscript.

Place	Date	Hour	Summary of Events and Information	Remarks and references to Appendices
	20/10/17.		No.2 Company to 18th.M.V.S.	
	21/10/17.		Fine day. Wire from No.1 Company re prospects of move. 1 surplus Rider from No.3 to No.2 Coy.	
	22/10/17.		Order received for T/Capt. F.M.Upson to proceed to England for course of Infantry training. Order issued to Coys to place 1 Limber each at disposal of Salvage Officer daily. 1.HD.horse, No.1 Company, to 44th. M.V.S.	
	23/10/17.		Wet day. Issued orders to Capt.Upson to leave on the 24th. Capt. Franks and Lt.Creer to No.1 Company to take over supplies. Received information that Lt. Mew was admitted to Hospital in England. 2/Lieut. Balmer transferred from No.4 to No.2 Company, 2/Lieut.Dwane No.1 to No.3 Coy., and 2/Lieut.Forbes No.2 to No.4 Coy. and to be Supply Officer. 2/Lieut. Carle evacuated to 44th. C.C.S. Lieut. Harris attached from No.4 to No.3 Company. "Daimler" sent to No.1 Coy.for move.	
	24/10/17.		Inspected 1st.LineTransport of 2nd.Royal Fusil's and 86th. Machine Gund Company.	
	25/10/17.		Went to DOULLENS to meet Headquarters Company arriving by rail from PROVEN AREA. Found no billets arranged, so went to Area Commandant and 3rd.Army H.Q. and arranged for billets at SARTON. Company arrive DOULLENS 5 p.m., 8 hours over scheduled time.	
	26/10/17.		Pte.Gomm,No.3 Coy., appointed Cpl. 2 Dr. and 1 Cpl. No.1 Coy. evacuated. 1 Cpl. from Base and posted to No.1 Coy.	

Army Form C. 2118.

WAR DIARY
or
INTELLIGENCE SUMMARY.
(Erase heading not required.)

Instructions regarding War Diaries and Intelligence Summaries are contained in F.S. Regs., Part II. and the Staff Manual respectively. Title pages will be prepared in manuscript.

Place	Date	Hour	Summary of Events and Information	Remarks and references to Appendices
	27/10/17.		5 Category "B" Clerks arrive, very little knowledge of military clerking.	
	28/10/17.		Railhead ARRAS. Supplies drawn by M.T. Orders received for Cpl.Shand to be attached to Infty. Bde, on probation for commission. 5 Cpls, 1 Clerk and 4 Drs. from Base and posted to Coys. Received notes	
	29/10/17.		Railhead ARRAS. To send Category "A" Clerks to Base on 31st.inst. Inspected 1st.Line Transport of Lancashire Fusiliers, Royal Guernsey Light Infantry and Middlesex Regiment.	
	30/10/17.		Railhead BOISLEUX. 2 Coys draw by M.T. and 1 by H.T. Leave allotment for November issued to Companies. Lieut. Harris sent back to No.4 Company.	
	31/10/17.		Fine day. Inspected No. 2 Company. Lines and Stabling; also Wagon Park nearly finished. Change over Sgt. Clarke and Cpl. Sands from No.1 Coy to No.2 Coy.	

Lieut.Colonel,A.S.C.,
Commg., 29th.Divisional Train.

29th. DIVISIONAL TRAIN.

WAR DIARY.

VOLUMN 22.

November, 1917.

Army Form C. 2118.

WAR DIARY
or
INTELLIGENCE SUMMARY.
(Erase heading not required.)

Instructions regarding War Diaries and Intelligence Summaries are contained in F.S. Regs., Part II. and the Staff Manual respectively. Title pages will be prepared in manuscript.

Place	Date	Hour	Summary of Events and Information	Remarks and references to Appendices
BLAIREVILLE	1/11/17.		Fine. T/2/Lieut.B.B.Garle struck off strength by Medical Board in England. Railhead at BOISIEUX au MONT.	
	2/11/17.		Fine. I visited No. 4 Coy. at BIENVILLERS. All Horses were under cover; but no NISSEN Huts yet received for men. Authority received from the BASE to promote supply N.C.Os to substantive rank.	
	3/11/17.		Fine.	
	4/11/17.		Fine. Dr.W.H.Taylor to 88th.Field Ambulance for duty.	
	5/11/17.		Fine. Train Headquarters moved to BERLES au BOIS. Lieut. L.C.Shadwell proceeded on leave to England. Dr.Arden T.H.Q. proceeded on Leave. Captain & Adjutant C.E.Browne rejoined T.H.Q. from Divisional Headquarters, "Q" Branch, on instructions from G.H.Q. at Deauville	
BERLES.	6/11/17.		S.S.O. to new area to make arrangements delivering supplies ∧ Dr.W.H.Smith admitted 89th. Field Ambulance.	
	7/11/17.		Wet. Inspected Newfoundland Transport. 2/Lieut. Bracegirdle joined from Base and posted to No.1 Coy. Dr. A.Skuse admitted to Hospital from leave in England.	
	8/11/17.		Dull. Dr.G.H. Crosby evacuated to 56th. C.C.S.	
	9/11/17.		Wet. Ptes. Grandorge and Hunt, Cpl.Grimshaw and Drs.Greave,Smaile,Head,Nelson, Knt Leigh,Reeves	

Army Form C. 2118.

WAR DIARY
or
INTELLIGENCE SUMMARY.
(Erase heading not required.)

Instructions regarding War Diaries and Intelligence Summaries are contained in F. S. Regs., Part II. and the Staff Manual respectively. Title pages will be prepared in manuscript.

Place	Date	Hour	Summary of Events and Information	Remarks and references to Appendices
	9/11/17.		Smith, W.F. and Taylor, arrived from BASE, and posted to Coys and Field Ambulances as required to complete Establishment. Transferred Ptes. Bone and Lavy to 61st.Divl.Train. 1 H.D. evacuated to M.V.S.	
	10/11/17.		Dull. Dr.Sadd. Wakefield evacuated to 3rd. Canadian Hospital. 1 G.S.Wagon received to replace one destroyed by shell fire. No.1 Coy. moved from MARIEUX to TREUX.	
	11/11/17.		Fine. Vauxhall Car returned from Workshops after inspection. Dr.Whr.Gilbert evacuated to 20th. C.C.S. Inspected 1st.Line Transport of 2/Hants Regt. Lieut.Blount proceeded on leave to England.	
	12/11/17.		No.1 Coy. received orders to move; car sent for S.O.Divl.Troops to make arrangements for journey en route. Interpreter Rossat rejoined from D.H.Q..	
	13/11/17.		Fine. S.S.O. sent to new area in advance. Dr.D.G.Lewis, No.1 Coy. died, heart failure. Instructions received for the Division to move to new area, very secret. Orders issued re screening of lights etc.	
	14/11/17.		Captains Crone and Franks return from PARIS leave. Sgt. Rogulski arrived from BASE and posted to No.3 Coy. No.1 Coy. moved to MANENCOURT.	
	15/11/17.		Fine. Lieut. W.E.C.Hulme proceeded on leave to England. Gifts received from A.S.C. Comforts Fund and	

Wt. W2544/1454 700,000 5/15 D. D. & L. A.D.S.S./Forms/C. 2118.

Army Form C. 2118.

WAR DIARY
or
INTELLIGENCE SUMMARY.
(Erase heading not required.)

Instructions regarding War Diaries and Intelligence Summaries are contained in F. S. Regs., Part II. and the Staff Manual respectively. Title pages will be prepared in manuscript.

Place	Date	Hour	Summary of Events and Information	Remarks and references to Appendices
	15/11/17.		Fund and distributed to Companies.	
	16/11/17.		Dull. 2 H.D. and 2 Riders received from Base Remounts. Bde.Companies move with Bde.Transport.	to BAPAUME
	17/11/17.		Dull. Vauxhall car to Workshops for repairs. Supplies issued to Units at Railhead and taken by them on rail to new area, PERONNE DISTRICT. Brigade Companies continue their march to ~~BAPAUME~~ MOISLAINS and HAUT-ALLAINES.	
	18/11/17.		Fine. Supplies drawn by Lorries from LA CHAPELLETTE, PERONNE, and dumped at EQUANCOURT for 86th. Bde.,FINS for 87th.Bde., and SOREL for 88th.Bde. No.refilling. Coys moved after dark to Camps at NURLU. Supplies for Artillery drawn from ROCQUINGNY. No.1 Coy at ETRICOURT. Advanced Dump established at VILLERS PLOUICH - 5,000 Preserved Meat and Biscuit Rations,5,000 Oats: Lieut. T.Dwane placed in charge. Train H.Q. moved from BERLES to NURLU.	
NURLU.	19/11/17.		Supplies for whole Division less Artillery for consumption 21st. drawn from FINS Railhead and loaded in bulk onto Decauville Railway and delivered to sidings at EQUANCOURT,FINS and SOREL for 86th.,87th.and 88th. Bdes. respectively. Supplies for consumption 20th. and 21st. issued in the afternoon. No.1 Company moved to NURLU Camp. Cpl.Crowe and Dr.Adderton to VI Corps Rest Station.	
	20/11/17.		Dull. Cpl.Shilton admitted to Hospital from leave in England. Supplies for consumption 22nd.	

Army Form C. 2118.

WAR DIARY
or
INTELLIGENCE SUMMARY.
(Erase heading not required.)

Instructions regarding War Diaries and Intelligence Summaries are contained in F. S. Regs., Part II. and the Staff Manual respectively. Title pages will be prepared in manuscript.

Place	Date	Hour	Summary of Events and Information	Remarks and references to Appendices
	20/11/17.		drawn from FINS and dumped at NEUDECOURT by Decauville. No refilling to-day.	
	21/11/17.			
	22/11/17.		Dull. 1 Riding horse lost in forward area at VILLERS PLOUICH. Major Gillam to Transport Duties No.1 Coy. Capt. Franks appointed A/S.S.O.	
	23/11/17.		Fine. Most of Train wagons were used to assist carrying ammunition to forward area. Lieut.L.C. Shadwell returned from leave.	
	24/11/17.		Dull. 1 H.D. evacuated to 18th.M.V.S.	
	25/11/17.		Fine. Cold. Train Transport employed on R.E.Work in Forward Area. Order received for T/Capt. W.A.B.Conran to proceed to Elstow School, England for Infantry training. 2/Lieut.F.W.Martin joined from BASE for duty and posted to No.1 Company.	
	26/11/17.		Fine. Cold. Capt.W.A.B.Conran left for England and struck off the strength.	
	27/11/17.		Dull. Lieut.W.H.King, proceeded on leave to England. Train Transport employed on R.E.Work in Forward Area. No.1 Company lost 1 G.S.Wagon destroyed by shell fire. Lieut. Shadwell acts as acts as Supply Officer for 87th.Bde.	
	28/11/17.		Fine. Train Transport employed on R.E. Work in Forward Area. Sgt.Frith returned from No.2 R.H.T. Depot at Blackheath, no instructions yet received as to his disposal.	

Army Form C. 2118.

WAR DIARY
or
INTELLIGENCE SUMMARY.
(Erase heading not required.)

Instructions regarding War Diaries and Intelligence Summaries are contained in F. S. Regs., Part II. and the Staff Manual respectively. Title pages will be prepared in manuscript.

Place	Date	Hour	Summary of Events and Information	Remarks and references to Appendices
	29/11/17.		Fine. Capt.R.C.O.Viveash proceeded to England on leave. Train Transport for R.E.Work in Forward Area. Supply Section for Artillery withdrawn from VILLERS PLOUICH to NURLU. Artillery Supplies dumped at Decauville Siding A.X.135.	
	30/11/17.		Fine. Train Transport detailed for work in forward area; but cancelled owing to operations. Supplies for Infantry taken by Train Vehicles to MARCOING and from there manhandled by Units to their lines. Other Units draw from NURLU. Supplies for Infantry for consumption 2nd. December taken by Decauville line to RIBECOURT and dumped with a Supply Officer and Issuers. Supplies for Artillery atvA.X.135 temporarily abandoned owing to sudden advance of the enemy. No.S/4/056698 S.Q.M.S. G.A.Perceval killed in action.	

1st.December,1917.

Lieut. Colonel,A.S.C.,
Commg.,29th.Divisional Train.

Army Form C. 2118.

29D Train
Vol 22

WAR DIARY
or
INTELLIGENCE SUMMARY.
(Erase heading not required.)

Place	Date	Hour	Summary of Events and Information	Remarks and references to Appendices
NURLU. (FINS area)	DEC. 1917. 1st.	—	Orders for move cancelled, and Train remains in the Fins area, pending further instructions. 10 Waggons on R.E. work at Marcoing.	
	2nd.	—	Line fully established before CAMBRAI once again, and all units settle down once again in their original camps.—	
	3rd.	—	8 Waggons on R.E. work at Marcoing and Masnieres. Warning order received for Division to move to the LE CAUROY area, move to be completed on a two day's "trek".	
	4th.		Preparations for move.	
	5th.		Brigades move off and stop in BAPAUME Area to pass night 5/6th. Aero-plane (enemy) activity during night, and bombs dropped in the neighbourhood of Bapaume. No.4 Coy had eight horses killed by bomb, and No.3 Coy. two. 1 G.S.Wagon destroyed also. TrainHeadquarters move to MANIN (LE CAUROY area) after staying the night in Bapaume Area.	
	6th.		No.3 Coy. reach their destination at LIENCOURT, No.2 Coy. arrive at HOUVIN and No.4 Coy. at SUS-ST.LEGER. Billets very bad in the 87th.Brigade (No.3 Coy's)area.	
MANIN.	7th.		Frosty and heavy snow fall during night – Train Headquarters open at MANIN. Railhead for all Brigades at FREVENT. Divisional Artillery move from the FINS Area to BAPAUME on the 1st. day's trek to the DOULLENS area. M.T. drawing Supplies for all the Infantry Brigades from Railhead.	

Army Form C. 2118.

WAR DIARY
or
INTELLIGENCE SUMMARY.
(Erase heading not required.)

Instructions regarding War Diaries and Intelligence Summaries are contained in F. S. Regs., Part II. and the Staff Manual respectively. Title pages will be prepared in manuscript.

Place	Date	Hour	Summary of Events and Information	Remarks and references to Appendices
MANIN.	Dec. 1917 10th.	-	Frosty - 2Lieut.W.J.C.Thorold reported for duty with the Train from the Base Depot,Havre,and posted to No.2 Company. One Private from the Base. Headquarters Company moves to TREUX.	
	11th.	-	Lieut.Hulme takes Command of No.3 Company during the absence of Captain Crone on leave to United Kingdom.	
	12th.	-	Remounts available for the Divisional Train at Remount Depot,ABBEVILLE. 1 Warrant Officer and 4 men from each Company detailed to fetch same. Captain Franks goes on leave to the United Kingdom and Adjutant takes over duties as S.S.O. during his absence.	
	13th.		Warning Order received for the Division (less Artillery) to move to the FRUGES area.	
	14th.		Orders issued to all Brigade Companies respecting the move to FRUGES area. Three day's "trek" to be made by each Company.	
	15th.		Order received for the move of the Divisional Artillery to the FRUGES Area.	
	16th.		No.2 Company move,with the 86th.Brigade to LIGNY-VACQUERIE on the first day's "trek".	
	17th.		2Lieut.J.H.Hollowell reported to the Divisional Train for duty from the Base,and is posted to No.1 Company.	

2353 Wt. W2544/1454 700,000 5/15 D.D.&L. A.D.S.S./Forms/C.2118.

Army Form C. 2118.

WAR DIARY
or
INTELLIGENCE SUMMARY.
(Erase heading not required.)

Instructions regarding War Diaries and Intelligence Summaries are contained in F.S. Regs., Part II. and the Staff Manual respectively. Title pages will be prepared in manuscript.

Place	Date	Hour	Summary of Events and Information	Remarks and references to Appendices
MANIN.	17th. (cont.d)		86th.Brigade (No.2 Company) move to VIEIL-HESDIN. 87th.Brigade (No.3 Company) move to LIGNY-VACQUERIE on the first day's "trek" to FRUGES area.	
	18th.	—	Train Headquarters move to HESDIN and stop there for night, en route for HUCQUELIERS. No.2 Company move with the 86th.Brigade, to RUMILLY, their destination in the FRUGES area. and No.3 Coy., reach VIEIL HESDIN on their second Day's trek. No.4 Company move with the 88th.Brigade to LIGNY-VACQUERIE on their first day's "trek".	
HESDIN	19th.	—	Train Headquarters "trek" to HUCQUELIERS, but owing to no billets being available have to return and seek billets in HESDIN. No.3 Company move to WAILLY their destination in the FRUGES area. NO4 COY. arrive at VIEIL-HESDIN on their second day's "trek". Railhead for the three Brigades HESDIN and Mechanical Transport draw Supplies to Dumps.	
	20th.	—	Hard frost— One S.Q.M.S. reported from the 36th.Division,in the place of S.Q.M.S.Perceval and posted to Headquarters Company. No.1 Company moves,by march route,to MARECHAL on the way to join the Division in the FRUGES area.	
	21st.	—	Very hard frost still prevailing,and great difficulties experienced with the horsed-transport.	
	23rd.	—	Authority received for one month's leave,granted to Commanding Officer,from 29th.Dec.1917 to 28th.January,1918.	

(M 5344/M/F 53) 100,000 5/15 D. D. & L.   A.D.S.S./Forms/C. 2118.

Army Form C. 2118.

WAR DIARY
or
INTELLIGENCE SUMMARY.
(Erase heading not required.)

Instructions regarding War Diaries and Intelligence Summaries are contained in F. S. Regs., Part II. and the Staff Manual respectively. Title pages will be prepared in manuscript.

Place	Date	Hour	Summary of Events and Information	Remarks and references to Appendices
HESDIN	24th.		Hard frost and deep snow. Preparations made for Xmas festivities for all ranks during Christmas Day. No.1 Coy.reaches CONTE, their destination in the FRUGES area. Christmas Greetings sent by the Commanding Officer to all Ranks. Christmas Dinners provided for all ranks. One wheeler arrived from the Base and posted to No.1 Coy.	
	25th.			
	28th.		Captain D. Franks resumes duties as S.S.O. having returned from leave.	
	29th.		Major Holman takes Command of the Train, during the absence of the Commanding Officer, on leave to the United Kingdom.	
	30th.		Orders received for the 87th.Brigade to move to the POPERINGHE area for work under the XIX Corps. One Corporal sent to the Base as surplus to establishment.	
	31st.		87th.Brigade move from WAILLY on first day's "trek" to new area. Railhead for this Brigade to be EDWARDSHOEK from to-morrow.	

Lieut.Colonel,A.S.C.
Commanding 29th.Divisional Train.

29th. DIVISIONAL TRAIN.

WAR DIARY
for the month of
January, 1918.

Army Form C. 2118.

WAR DIARY
or
INTELLIGENCE SUMMARY.
(Erase heading not required.)

Instructions regarding War Diaries and Intelligence Summaries are contained in F.S. Regs., Part II. and the Staff Manual respectively. Title pages will be prepared in manuscript.

Place	Date	Hour	Summary of Events and Information	Remarks and references to Appendices
HESDIN	1st/1/18.		Frosty. Warning order received re move of 29th. Division to TILQUES AREA.	
	2/1/18.		Preparations for move by all Units.	
	3/1/18.		Division less 87th.Bde. on move to TILQUES AREA. Move completed in one day. [illegible]	
	4/1/18.		Train H.Q. move from HESDIN to WIZERNES. D.H.Q. move to WIZERNES.	
WIZERNES	5/1/18.		Train Office opens in new area. New Year Honours published as follows :- Capt. & Adjt. G.E.Browne, M.C., 1/c SSM G.A.Fowle, M.S.M., Capt. F.M.Upson, Mentioned in Despatches, T/18525 A/SSM T.Mole, M.S.M. [illegible], T4/042154 A/Sgt. Hughes,J., mentioned in Despatches. No. S4/056703 A/Sgt. S.J.H. Rowe, M.M. for Gallant conduct at Cambrai operations.	
	6/1/18.		1 Driver from Base to No. 2 Company.	
	8/1/18.		Notice of Artillery moving.	
	9/1/18.		Warning Order of Artillery moving.	
	10/1/18.		Remounts available at CALAIS - Lt. Thorold and 6 men detailed to fetch same.	
	11/1/18.		Thaw precautions to come into force. No.1 Company on "Trek" with Artillery, staging night at ANCIENNE-ABBAYE WOESTINE.	
	12/1/18.		Warm & Rain. Thaw precautions in force from 11a.m. G.S.Wagons draw from Railhead. No.2 Company	

Army Form C. 2118.

WAR DIARY
or
INTELLIGENCE SUMMARY.
(Erase heading not required.)

Instructions regarding War Diaries and Intelligence Summaries are contained in F. S. Regs., Part II. and the Staff Manual respectively. Title pages will be prepared in manuscript.

Place	Date	Hour	Summary of Events and Information	Remarks and references to Appendices
	13/1/18.		provided 20 Wagons for drawing No.1 Company Forrage, the latter Company being on move to STEENVOORDE. Golder. G.S.Wagons continue to draw from Railhead. L Issuer and 3 Drivers from Base.	
	14/1/18.		Snow and Frost. Notification received that lorries will draw from Railhead on 15th. & 16th. New preparations for Thaw Precautions to be made. 1 Limber sent to Reinforcement Camp at BAILLEUX	
	15/1/18.		Snow & Rain. No. 2 Company moves to POPERINGHE - 1st.days trek. Wire received from Division asking for Categories of W.Os., N.C.Os and Men of Train.	
	16/1/18.		Train H.Q. moves to EDWARDSHOEK. Thaw precautions again in force. No.4 Company moves from QUECAMP for POPERINGHE - 1st. day trek.	
	17/1/18.		xxxx. xxxxxxxxxxxxxxxxxxxxxxxxxxxxxxxxxxxxxxxxxxxxxxxxxxNo.2 Coyxxx x xxxxxxxxxxxx xxxxxxxxxxxxxxxxxxxxxxxxxxx Fine. No. 4 Company arrives at EDWARDSHOCK,location Sheet 28, G.4.d.Cetral. Railhead for all fixed for VLAMERTINGHE.	
	18/1/18.		Fine. No.3 Company arroves at Sheet, 28, G.5.c.9.0. beside No.2 Company(Camps taken over by Companies in bad condition)	
	19/1/18.		Signals Move to MERSEY CAMP. Classification of O.R. of No.3 Company. 50 Chinese promised for work with Train.	

2353 Wt.W2514/1451 700,000 5/15 D. D. & L. A.D.S.S./Forms/C. 2118.

Army Form C. 2118.

WAR DIARY
or
INTELLIGENCE SUMMARY.
(Erase heading not required.)

Instructions regarding War Diaries and Intelligence Summaries are contained in F.S. Regs., Part II. and the Staff Manual respectively. Title pages will be prepared in manuscript.

Place	Date	Hour	Summary of Events and Information	Remarks and references to Appendices
	20/1/18.		Lt. Forbes returned off leave.	
	21/1/18.		Farrier from 5th. Aux.H.T.Company. No.1 Company takes over stables at G.4.b.5.1. Personnel of No.4 Coy., Classified.	
	22/1/18.		120 Tons of Coal arrive at Railhead. 50 Chineese report for work with Train, until 31st.inst. Leave allotment received for men of 226th. Employment Company attached to Train Companies. Personnel of No.2 Company classified.	
	24/1/18.		88th. Bde. relieved the 86th.Bde in the Line, latter go into supports.	
	25/1/18.		xxxxx Chinese Labour party increased to 100 O.R.	
	29/1/18.		80 Tons of Coal arrive at VLAMERTINGHE Railhead, 6 wagons on R.E.Work.	
	30/1/18.		Colonel Wright granted extension of leave to 3rd.February. 1 Issuer from Base to No.3 Company. Sugar allowance for Soldiers on leave reduced to 1 Oz.	
	31/1/18.		Time of drawing at Railhead altered. Warning Wire received that Royal Inniskilling Fusil. will probably leave the Division by rail on the 3rd. or 4th. for 36th.Division, and the Essex Regt. by march route to 37th. Division- Train xxxxxxxx Transport to accompany.	

for Lieut. Colonel, A.S.C.,
Commg., 29th. Divisional Train.

Major,

Army Form C. 2118.

WAR DIARY
or
INTELLIGENCE SUMMARY.
(Erase heading not required.)

29th. DIVISIONAL TRAIN, A.S.C.

WO 24

Place	Date	Hour	Summary of Events and Information	Remarks and references to Appendices
POPERINGHE.	FEB. 1st.	-	FINE-Visit of Staff Officers of the French Administrative Staff, to the Railhead at VLAMERTINGHE, to see the loading of Supplies, and Refilling Point of the Brigade Group at 29/H.14 b.6.9. Major F.H.A.Mayers reported for Duty with the 29th.Divisional Train,from the Base CALAIS.	
	2nd.		5 Drivers arrive from the Base-3 taken on the strength of the Train and 2 sent to the Field Ambulances. One Private Issuer appointed A/Cpl.Issuer. Captain C.G.Taylor proceeded on Leave to the United Kingdom. 2/Lieut. Martin became attached to the Central Purchase Board, G.H.Q., for Temporary Duty.	
	3rd.		Commanding Officer returned from Leave. A.D.M.S. wishes to have innoculated all ranks who have not been done during the past 12 months.	
	4th.		FINE. Daimler Car, Pte.Millichamp,Pte.Fernley,and Private Leith. sent to the Central Purchase Board for Temporary Duty. 6 G.S.Waggons on R.E. work in the Forward area. Arrangements made to send Inspection of all Companies billets by the Commanding Officer. 20 men daily to the Field Ambulances for Innoculation.	
	5th.		FINE- 6 Waggons on R.E. work in the Forward area. 40 Tons of coal arrive at Railhead,and cleared by Mechanical Transport. Sergeant reverted by Sentence of F.G.C.M.and transferred to the 89th.Field Ambulance. 8 Waggons leave the Train for attachment to the Royal Inniskilling Fusiliers,and Essex Regiment. (4 with each Unit).	

Army Form C. 2118.

WAR DIARY
or
INTELLIGENCE SUMMARY.
(Erase heading not required.)

29th. DIVISIONAL TRAIN.

Instructions regarding War Diaries and Intelligence Summaries are contained in F.S. Regs., Part II. and the Staff Manual respectively. Title pages will be prepared in manuscript.

Place	Date	Hour	Summary of Events and Information	Remarks and references to Appendices
POPERINGHE	6th.	-	FINE - Quantity of wood fuel cut near YPRES for issue - Remounts arrive at CALAIS for Divisional Train, including 2 Riders, 3 L.D., and 10 H.D.Horses.	
	7th.	-	STRONG WIND BLOWING. Major K.R.Holman granted a Special leave to United Kingdom. 8 Waggons on R.E. work in the Forward Area. Notification that Capt.Newton (O.C.4 Coy) has been granted an extension of leave, awaiting a Medical Board. Train required to render an availability state to the S.M.T.O., for the purpose of showing the amount of Transport available for use of the Corps.	
	8th.		WET. Notification received that the 3 Brigades move to the rest area on 11th. & 12 insts. 1 G.S.limber attached to the 918 Garrison Guard Company for Temporary Duty, from No.1 Coy. Captain C.Blount takes Command of No.4 Coy., during the absence of Capt.Newton.	
	9th.		FINE-DRY. Orders issued for move of 87th.Brigade. Farrier sent to the VIII Corps School from No.1 Coy. T2/Lieut.Wells transferred to No.2 Coy.	
	10th.		SHOWERY- 87th.Brigade move to WATOU rest area, and No.3 Coy.Train located near ABEELE. Major Mayers takes Temporary Command of No.1 Company during the absence of Major Holman. Instructions received for other two Companies (86th. & 88th.Brigades) and Train Headquarters to move to rest area. Orders received also for the move of the Divisional Artillery.	
	11th.		Remounts arrive from CALAIS, for Distribution to the Divisional Train, from No.1 Company's lines.	

Army Form C. 2118.

WAR DIARY
or
INTELLIGENCE SUMMARY.
(Erase heading not required.)

29th. Divisional Train.

Instructions regarding War Diaries and Intelligence Summaries are contained in F. S. Regs., Part II. and the Staff Manual respectively. Title pages will be prepared in manuscript.

Place	Date	Hour	Summary of Events and Information	Remarks and references to Appendices
	11th./2/18.		No.2 and No.4 Companies move with 86th. and 88th. Bdes. T.H.Q. move to STEENVOORDE taking over from the 8th. Division.	
STEENVOORDE	12th./2/18.		T.H.Q. open at STEENVOORDE. 1 Pte.(Issuer) and 4 Drivers from the Base as reinforcements. The 4 Machine Gun Coys of the Division formed into a Machine Gun Battalion.	
	13th./2/18.		Wet. Agricultural Officer asks for two pairs of horses to assist in Farming work in this Area. Report rendered to Headquarters "Q" on the filthy state of the Camps taken over by Brigade Companies.	
	14th./2/18.		Fine. Instructions given to No.4 Company to supply 2 pairs of horses for ploughing purposes to Agricultural Officer. No. 1 Company move with Divisional Artillery from G.4.b.6.1. to A.26.b.0.7. (Sheet 28.) Camp taken over by No.1 Company from No.1 Comapny, 8th.Division? Train in a very bad state.	
	15th./2/18.		Fine. Showers of wood fuel, party of ten Royal Newfoundland Regt. are ** is detailed to cut wood at WIPPENHOEK Railhead.	
	16th./2/18.		Fine. Order received re move of 88th.Bde from WINNEZEELE to POPERINGHE Area on the 19th. to relieve the 86th. Bde. at POPERINGHE. 86th. Bde to camp at EECHE Area.	
	16th./2/18.		Fine. Owing to roads in WINNEZEELE and EECHE being out of bounds to Mechanical Transport the	

Army Form C. 2118.

WAR DIARY
or
INTELLIGENCE SUMMARY.

29th. Divisional Train.

(Erase heading not required.)

Instructions regarding War Diaries and Intelligence Summaries are contained in F.S. Regs., Part II. and the Staff Manual respectively. Title pages will be prepared in manuscript.

Place	Date	Hour	Summary of Events and Information	Remarks and references to Appendices
	18th/2/18. (Contd)		Refilling Points of Nos 2 and 4 Groups are ordered to move to a more suitable location at 27/K.32.d.41. G.O. approved of this site. Capt. & Adjt. C.E.Browne,M.C. granted leave to U.K. from 18th/2/18 to 20/3/18.	
	19th/2/18.		Nos. 2 and 4 Groups move to new refilling point. 88th.Bde march to POPERINGHE Area and relieve the 86th.Bde who march to BECKE Area. Detachment of waggons from No.4 Company relieves detachment from No. 2 Company at No.1 Company's lines.	
	20th./2/18.		Nos. 2 and 4 Groups Refilling points again move to more suitable site oposite STEENVOORDE Railway Station. 1 lorry detailed to bring kits from Reinforcement Camp at XXX BAILLEUL to No.2 Company's Refilling Point, at STEENVOORDE, and 1 G.S.Wagon detailed by each Brigade Company to collect from Refilling Point and deliver to their respective Brigades.	
	21st/2/18.		2 Riders and 1 groom temporarily attached to Corps Agricultural Officer. STEENVOORDE.	
	24th./2/18.		Fine. 120 Tons of coal arrive for Division at WIPPENHOEK Railhead.T/Capt. L.Newton, struck off the strength from 7/2/18.	
	25th/2/18.		Orders issued respecting move of 87th.Bde to POPERINGHE area in relief of 88th.Bde.	
	26th/2/18.		1 Sgt. from BASE and Posted to No.1 Company. 5 H.T. Drivers from Base and posted to 89th. Field Ambulance. 87th.Bde. move to POPERINGE Area ad 88th. Bde. return to WENNEZEELE Area.	

Army Form C. 2118.

WAR DIARY
or
INTELLIGENCE SUMMARY.

29th. Divisional Train.

(Erase heading not required.)

Place	Date	Hour	Summary of Events and Information	Remarks and references to Appendices
	(Contd)			
	26th./2/18.		87th.Bde. Supply and Baggage Wagons relieve those of 86th.Bde. attached to No.1 Company.	
	27th./2/18.		Major Mayors posted to No.3 Company to take Command. 4 Wagons of the Royal Innis.Fusiliers to No. 3 Company.	
	28th/2/18.		1 HT. Sgt. transferred to the Supply, under Authority of A.S.C. Section.	

Lieut. Colonel, A.S.C.,
Comm&., 29th.Divisional Train.

War Diary

29 Div. Train

1—31 March

1918.

Vol 25

Army Form C. 2118.

Instructions regarding War Diaries and Intelligence
Summaries are contained in F.S. Regs. Part II.
and the Staff Manual respectively. Title pages
will be prepared in manuscript.

WAR DIARY
or
INTELLIGENCE SUMMARY.
(Erase heading not required.)

29TH. DIVISIONAL TRAIN

MARCH-1918.

Place	Date	Hour	Summary of Events and Information	Remarks and references to Appendices
STEENVOORDE	March 1st.	—	FINE. Four waggons of the Essex Regiment Transport return to No.4 Company. from the 37th. Divisional Train.	
	2nd.	—	Farr.S.Sgt.Simmill (No.TS.10354) struck off the Strength, having been evacuated to the 3rd. Canadian General Hospital 14-1-18. Orders received regarding the forth-coming move to the POPERINGHE area.	
	3rd.	—	FINE.-- Move Orders sent to the 3 Brigade Companies.	
	4th.	—	FINE.-- The two riders attached to the Corps Agricultural Officer, withdrawn, also the waggon detailed for Sanitary Work in STEENVOORDE cancelled, owing to move.	
	5th.	—	No.4 Company and No.3 Company (88th.& 87th. Bdes) move to the new area. Sheet 28 NW. Location G.4.a.1.1. viz. RYDE CAMP, and EDWARDSHOEK.	
	6th.	—	FINE.-- Train Headquarters move to EDWARDSHOEK 28(G.4 b.6.1.) and No.2 Company (86th.Bde.) to RYDE CAMP. from EECKE.	
POPERINGHE	7th.	—	FINE.-- Daily detail received from the Bath's Officer at VLAMERTINGHE for 3 waggons to report at 8-0 a.m. each morning. Reinforcements arrive and are posted as follows:-- T4/033170 Dr.Rankin S. to 89th.F.Ambulance. T3/320 " Fry W.E. " " " T2/017392 " Savage D.E. " " " T/21283 " Streamen F.C. to No.4 Company. T4/043847 " Whitehead E. " " 2 "	
	8th.	—	FINE. TO Reinforcements from Base:-- T3/340736 Dr.Vickery H. posted to No.4 Company. T4/071072 " Pettican C. " " No.2 " T/326045 " Williams J.M. " " 89th.F.Ambulance. T/337567 " Berry H. " " " T/325670 " Child C. " " " T/294671 " Doyle H. " " " T/3629 [illegible] " [illegible] " " "	

H.Q.
29TH DIV'L TRAIN
No. D1/28
Date.

Army Form C. 2118.

WAR DIARY
29TH. DIVISIONAL TRAIN.
or
INTELLIGENCE SUMMARY.

(Erase heading not required.)

MARCH 1918.

Place	Date	Hour	Summary of Events and Information	Remarks and references to Appendices
POPERINGHE	8th.	-	(Continued) T/309664 Dr.McGuire to 89th.F.Ambulance. T/364714 " Jacob E.W. 88th. "	
	9th.	-	Return, for suggestions for economising Personnel, Animals, and Transport, Stores etc. in connection with the authorised Establishment of a Divisional Train, called for, by Division.	
	10th.	-	FINE-- T3/023729 Sgt.WILLIAMSON W. (No.2 Company) detailed to attend a Course on the Hotchkiss Machine Gun, for Anti-aircraft work, at the VIII Corps School. System of Lectures organised in the Companies, on Economy. Commanding Officer inspects the 86th.& 88th.First-Line Transport.	
	11th.	-	One Limber detached from No.3 Company, to the 918 Garrison Guard Company, for temporary duty whilst the Division is in this area.	
	12th.	-	Notification received that the 86th.Bde. relieve the 88th.Bde. in the line--50 tons of coal arrive at Railhead for Divisional Fuel Dump--T4/250897 Farr.Cpl.Reynard G. taken on the Strength of No.1 Company from 49th.Divisional Train.	
	13th.	-	FINE-- Remounts arrive at CALAIS to-morrow; Orders issued to fetch same, and LT.J.C.THOROLD to take charge of the party. General Sir Beauvoir de Lisle, leaves the Division to take command of the XIII Corps.	
	14th.	-	WET-Party leaves POPERINGHE to collect Remounts from No.5 Remount Depot CALAIS	
	16th.	-	S4/056848 Pte.W.GOSDEN sent to the Base, surplus to Establishment	
	17th.	-	FINE-- Remounts arrive from CALAIS, and are distributed to the various Companies.	
	18th.	-	FINE-- Reinforcements arrive from the Base and are posted as follows:-- TS/8362 A/Farr.S.Sgt.HURREN A. to No,1 Company T/331157 Dr. " Pearson J. " 88th.F.Ambulance. T3/023378 " " Perry J. " 89th. " T/327388 " " Pinder T. " " "	

WAR DIARY
or
INTELLIGENCE SUMMARY.
(Erase heading not required.)

Army Form C. 2118.

29th. Divisional Train.

March, 1918.

Instructions regarding War Diaries and Intelligence Summaries are contained in F.S. Regs., Part II. and the Staff Manual respectively. Title pages will be prepared in manuscript.

Place	Date	Hour	Summary of Events and Information	Remarks and references to Appendices
	18/3/18.		(CONTINUED) T/331157 Dr. Pearson,J. to 88th. Field Ambulance.	
	19/3/18.		4 H.D. killed by shell fire of No.2 Company on Lancs. Fusiliers Lines. T4/056902 Dr.Far.Sharpe,E. sent to Base, Surplus to Establishment, from No.1 Company.	
	20/3/18.		Wet. 2 H.D. hit by shell outside D.A.D.O.S. Store at VLAMERTINGHE. One killed and one severely wounded. These animals were attached to No.2 Company from 87th. Divisional Train, East Lancs.	
	21/3/18.		Fine. T4/044056 Sgt. Freestone,H.C., No.1 Company, sent to VIII Corps Sanitation School for weeks course. 5 G.S. Wagons detailed to carry bricks from PACIFIC Siding to HAMHOEK.	
	22/3/18.		Captain and Adjutant C.E.Browne returns from leave. 88th. Brigade relieves the 87th.Bde. in the line; the 86th. Brigade going into support.	
	23/3/18.		Fine. Two G.S. Wagons from each Brigade Company to be temporarily attached to 1/2 Monmouth Regiment, with a Sergeant of No.4 Company in charge to convey bricks daily to WATERLOO.	
	24/3/18.		Fine. A small violet coloured air balloon fell in No.4 Company Camp, was brought to Train Headquarters and sent from there to Chemical Adviser,VIII Corps. Headquarters "Q" wire. "All Leave cancelled until further orders". Opening of great German Offensive on the SOMME.	
	25/3/18.		Fine. Eight wagon loads of wood drawn from Bilge Dump to Divisional Fuel Dump at Vlamertinghe.	
	26/3/18.		Dry and very cold. T/2nd.S.S.Lockwood,A.S.C., reported from Base Depot to be attached to the Train and posted to No.2 Company. 100 Tons of Coal arrived at VLAMERTINGHE Railhead for the Division and cleared to Divisional Fuel Dump by Train Transport.	
	27/3/18.		The 88th. Brigade relieve the 87th. Brigade in the line.	
	28/3/18.		No.2 group and No.3 group change Refilling points. Location of No.2 Group, 28/H.14.b.6.9. and No.3 Group 28/H.6.b.4.9. Ten wagon loads of wood drawn from near BILGE Dump.	
	29/3/18.		T4/160915 Dr. Lewis,J.W.R., No.4 Company detailed to attend Sanitation Course at VIII Corps School for one week.	
	31/3/18.		Six wagons sent to relieve those at present attached to 1/2 Monmouth Regt. Notification received that remounts are available at CALAIS on 2nd. prox. Order received for extension of Divisional Fighting Front; an 86th.Brigade to relieve the 88th.Brigade.	

Lieut.Colonel,A.S.C.,
Commg., 29th. Divisional Train.

29th. DIVISIONAL TRAIN.

WAR DIARY
for
APRIL, 1918.
--o--

Army Form C. 2118.

WAR DIARY
or
INTELLIGENCE SUMMARY.

(Erase heading not required.)

29th. DIVISIONAL TRAIN.

Instructions regarding War Diaries and Intelligence Summaries are contained in F.S. Regs. Part II. and the Staff Manual respectively. Title pages will be prepared in manuscript.

Place	Date	Hour	Summary of Events and Information	Remarks and references to Appendices
BRANDHOEK	1st./4/18.		1 Rider and 4 H.D. from No.5 Base Remount Depot, CALAIS. Railhead VLAMERTINGHE. Feeding strength 18,727. Supplies drawn by H.T.	
	2nd./4/18.		3 wagons of Surplus Transport detached for a week to H.Q. 49th.A.F.A. Bde. Number of Petrol Cans filled with Water and conveyed to 87th. and 88th. Bde H.Q. at DEADEND. 50 tons of Coal cleared by Train Transport to Divisional Fuel Dump. Feeding strength 18,125.	
	3rd./4/18.		Showery. T4/146779 Dr. Kingswell,H.J.(No.4 Coy.) evacuated to 3rd. Aus.C.C.S. as result of an accident. Feeding strength 17,720.	
	4th./4/18.		Feeding Strength 17,607. 1008 lbs. bran, 9400 lbs linseed cake and 168 lbs linseed drawn.	
	5th./4/18.		S/312220 Pte. Locton,J.G. reported from A.S.C. Base Depot Havre and posted to No. 4 Company. All Surplus Transport, including 4 G.S.Wagons attached to Divisional Train of each of the following units :- Essex Regt., Inniskilling Fusiliers, East Lancs.Regt. and Middlesex Regt, warned to be to be prepared to move off to unknown destination at 6 hours notice from 6 a.m. to-morrow. (6th.inst.) Feeding Strength 19,199.	
	6th./4/18.		Wet. Orders received for relief of 86th. Bde in Line. Feeding Strength 18,761.	
	7th./4/18.		Warning Order received for move - 87th. Bde to move on 8th. to WATOU Area and 88th.Bde on 9th. to same Area. Instructions sent to Companies to place spare stores in Divisional Store at	

Army Form C. 2118.

WAR DIARY
INTELLIGENCE SUMMARY.

29th. DIVISIONAL TRAIN.

(Erase heading not required.)

Instructions regarding War Diaries and Intelligence Summaries are contained in F.S. Regs., Part II. and the Staff Manual respectively. Title pages will be prepared in manuscript.

Place	Date	Hour	Summary of Events and Information	Remarks and references to Appendices
POPERINGHE.	7th/4/18.		T/25140 Dr. Fox G., and T/33308 Dr. Brazier,J.R. from A.S.C.,Base Depot on 7-4-1918 and posted to Nos 2 and 4 Coys respectively. T/23416 Dr. Richardson sent from No. 1 Company to No. 2 Company to complete Surplus Transport. All Surplus Transport sent to join VIII Corps Surplus Transport. (Athy. 29th.Div.No. 684/48 dated 6/4/18.	
	8th/4/18.		Orders received for move by rail to join XIII Corps, Companies notified. 87th.Brigade. move to WATOU Area. 4 of the Surplus wagons recalled and 2 posted to No. 4 Company and 2 to No. 2 Company. Feeding Strength 17,962.	
	9th/4/18.		Entrainment Orders cancelled. Nos.2 and 3 Companies march to VIEUX-BERQUIN on night 9th/10th to join XV Corps. Feeding Strength 16,806.	
	10th/4/18.		No. 4 Company march to VIEUX-BERQUIN and Train Headquarters to LE PARC in Foret de NIEPPE. Feeding strength 16748. Supplies drawn by M.T. and conveyed to refilling points at VIEUX-BERQUIN. Divisional Artillery with No.1 Company and proportion of Supply Lorries remain at EDWARDSHOEK and draw in future through 41st.Divisional Train.	
	11th/4/18.		Train Headquarters move to MORBECQUE and Brigade Companies to STRAZEELE. Feeding strength 14,352. Supplies drawn by M.T. - Railhead STRAZEELE.	
	12th/4/18.		On night 11th/12th. Train Headquarter Transport move to STAPLE, Commanding Officer,Adjutant and S.S.O. move with cars to Divisional Headquarters, LE MOTTE. The 3 Brigade Companies move	

Army Form C. 2118.

WAR DIARY
or
~~INTELLIGENCE SUMMARY~~   29th. DIVISIONAL TRAIN.
(Erase heading not required.)

Instructions regarding War Diaries and Intelligence Summaries are contained in F. S. Regs., Part II. and the Staff Manual respectively. Title pages will be prepared in manuscript.

Place	Date	Hour	Summary of Events and Information	Remarks and references to Appendices
	12th/4/18.		into BORRE Area. Feeding Strength 12,242. Railhead EBBLINGHAM.	
	14th/4/18.		Train Headquarters move to HONDEGHEM. No.3 Company just outside same village. No.4 Company move to STEENVOORDE and No.2 Company to ST.MARIE CAPPEL near CASSEL. Strength 6,666	
	16th/4/18.		TS/4271 Dr.Far.Weller,No.1 Company, sent to Base as Surplus to Establishment. Orders received for move of Division, less Artillery, No.3 Company to ~~rearkxxx~~ go to rear area, No.2 Company to remain at HONDEGHEM to feed to composite Brigade in Line. No.4 Company remain at STEENVOORDE. Feeding Strength 8446.	
	17th/4/18.		No.3 Company move back to CAMPAGNE nr.ST-OMER. Train Headquarters remain at HONDEGHEM. Feeding Strength 10419. C.O.,Adjutant,and S.S.O. proceed to D.H.Q. at ST.SYLVESTRE CAPPEL.	
	18th/4/18.		Locations:-No.2 Coy.,at HONDEGHEM,No.3 Coy.,at CAMPAGNE,No.4 Coy.,at STEENVOORDE. Feeding Strength 10,112.	
	19th/4/18.		Authority received to take T/2nd.Lieut.S.S.Lockwood on strength of Unit, and is posted to No.3 Company, 2/4/18(Athy. A.S.C.,G.H.Q./1996O/2 d/- 7.4.18. T4/158094 Dr. Sheeran,J., No.1 Company, evacuated sick to C.C.S., 14/4/18. Feeding Strength 10,378.	
	20th/4/18.		Divisional Headquarters move from ST. SYLVESTRE CAPPEL to HONDEGHEM. Feeding Strength 9,918.	
	21st./4/18.		No.3 Company move from CAMPAGNE to LONGUE CROIX. 27/U.5.c.2.4. No.4 Company move from STEENVOORDE to 27/U.10.c.2.5. near STAPLE. Feeding Strength 9,626. Order received from	

Army Form C. 2118.

WAR DIARY
or
~~INTELLIGENCE~~ SUMMARY.

29th. DIVISIONAL TRAIN.

(Erase heading not required.)

Instructions regarding War Diaries and Intelligence Summaries are contained in F.S. Regs., Part II. and the Staff Manual respectively. Title pages will be prepared in manuscript.

Place	Date	Hour	Summary of Events and Information	Remarks and references to Appendices
	21st/4/18.		Division to dump supplies of day in hand at M.T.Companies location. All drawing from Railhead to be by H.T. as lorries are required by Corps. All fresh meat has been issued and a corresponding quantity of P.M. replaced at M.T. Coy's Dump.	
	22nd/4/18.		Feeding Strength 9,927.	
	23rd/4/18		H.T. draw from EBBLINGHEM Railhead and deliver supplies to Units. ~~XX/XXXX~~ S4/056695 S.Sgt. Cooper, No.1 Company (attached No.4 Coy) and T1/2846 Cpl.Tidby, No.4 Company wounded by bomb from hostile aeroplane; also 10 H.D. horses wounded in nO.4 Company's Camp near STAPLE. Feeding Strength 10,156.	
	24th/4/18.		S.Sgt.Cooper and Cpl.Tidby evacuated to C.C.S. 5 H.D. horses of No.4 Company evacuated with wounds to 18th.M.V.S.. 5 reinforcements arrive from the A.S.C.Base Depot and are posted as follows :- T/260058 Dr. Dunn,F.S. ~~T4/XXXXXXXXXXXXXXXXX~~ to 88th.Field Ambulance. T/362255 Dr.Gauley,F. to 89th. Field Ambulance. T4/ 215067 Dr. Figgures,E.C. and T4/236200 Dr. Flood,E.S. to No. 2 Company. T/343219 Dr. Hardy,W.H. to No. 4 Company. Feeding Strength 11496.	
	25th./4/18		Feeding Strength 11422.	
	26th./4/18		The 4 G.S. Wagons of 1st.Royal Newfoundland Regt. leave the Division with that Unit and are replaced by 4 from 16th. Divisional Train, transport for Royal Dublin Fusiliers. Move order received for Divisional move to forward area. Supplies dumped at M.T. Coy's Camp are	

Army Form C. 2118.

WAR DIARY
or
INTELLIGENCE SUMMARY.   29th. DIVISIONAL TRAIN.
(Erase heading not required.)

Place	Date	Hour	Summary of Events and Information	Remarks and references to Appendices
	26th/4/18.		brought up by M.T. are refilled for delivery early to-morrow. After delivering supply wagons will proceed to Railhead, draw and refill, remaining loaded overnight. Feeding Strength 11,328.	
	28th/4/18.		Divisional Move takes place from HONDEGHEM Area to Forward Area. Train Headquarters and the 3 Brigade Companies move to WALLON CAPPEL and take over billets and camps from 31st.Divisional Train. Feeding Strength 12,720.	
	29th/4/18.		The 3 Brigade Refilling Points established in respective Company Lines. 1 H.D. Horse evacuated by No. 2 Company to 18th. M.V.S.	
	30th/4/18.		One of No1 Company's H.D. Horses, attached to No.2 Company, evacuated to 18th. M.V.S.	

Lieut. Colonel, A.S.C.,
Commg., 29th.Divisional Train.

29th. DIVISIONAL TRAIN.

WAR DIARY

for
the month of

May, 1918.

Army Form C. 2118.

WAR DIARY
or
INTELLIGENCE SUMMARY.

29th. Divisional Train.

(Erase heading not required.)

Instructions regarding War Diaries and Intelligence Summaries are contained in F.S. Regs., Part II. and the Staff Manual respectively. Title pages will be prepared in manuscript.

Place	Date	Hour	Summary of Events and Information	Remarks and references to Appendices
WALLON CAPPEL.	1/5/18.		Fine. T4/090416 L/Cpl. Cummimgs, No. 4 Coy., appointed A/Cpl. and transferred to No. 1 Coy to fill vacancy vice A/Cpl. Squires. T4/043832 Dr. Harbach,J., appointed A/L/Cpl. with pay, vice L/Cpl. Cummings and transferred to No. 4 Coy. Feeding Strength 11,079.	
	2/5/18.		Last Railhead drawing from EBBLINGHEM. Feeding Strength 13,546.	
	3/5/18.		Railhead now WARDRECQUES. Horse Transport drawing and delivering supplies. Feeding Strength 12,266.	
	4/5/18.		Notification received that T/Captain A.S. LEE, has been instructed to report for duty from 36th. Divisional Train. Feeding Strength 14,973	
	5/5/18.		Wet. 88th. Brigade relieved the 87th. Bde., in the line. T4/093107 Dr. Biggins,J., No. 2 Coy transferred to 86th. Brigade H.Q. T/307214 Pte. Kelly, J. evacuated sick to No. 2 C.C.S. Feeding strength 12,632.	
	6/5/18.		15 H.D. horses drawn from S.A.A. Section and taken on the strength. Feeding Strength 12,632.	
	7/5/18.		Fine. 2 Reinforcements arrive from A.S.C. Base Depot and are posted as follows :- T2/12577 Dr. Jones, T. to No. 4 Coy. T/330457 Dr. Martin, J.L. to 89th. Field Ambulance. Feeding Strength 14,844.	
	8/5/18.		Fine. T4/045067 Dr. Whr. Smith R.P., No. 3 Coy. on probation with R.F.C., as joiner, struck off the strength from 27/2/18. T4/042977 L/Cpl. Robertson, J. evacuated to Hospital and struck off the strength 1/5/18. 1. H.D. horse evacuated to 18th.M.V.S. from No. 4 Coy. Feeding Strength 14, 753.	

Army Form C. 2118.

WAR DIARY
or
INTELLIGENCE SUMMARY.   29th. Divisional Train.
(Erase heading not required.)

Instructions regarding War Diaries and Intelligence Summaries are contained in F.S. Regs., Part II. and the Staff Manual respectively. Title pages will be prepared in manuscript.

Place	Date	Hour	Summary of Events and Information	Remarks and references to Appendices
	9/5/18.		Fine. Transfers :- T4/034690 Dr. Dunford E., from D.H.Q. to No.1 Coy. T4/036914 Dr.Gittins,J., from No.1 Coy. to D.H.Q. Feeding Strength 14,949. T4/043832 A/L/Cpl. Harbach,J., and T/343219 Dr. Hardy, W.H. evacuated sick to 15th. C.C.S. from No.4 Company.	
	10/5/18.		Fine. Feeding Strength 14, 944. T1/4138 Dr. Lawrie,T. evacuated to 15th. C.C.S. from No.4 Company. T4/247466 Dr. Whr. Price, E., evacuated to No. 2 C.C.S., from No. 4 Company. T3/027177 Dr. Warren, W.J., evacuated to No. 2 C.C.S., from No. 4 Company.	
	11/5/18.		T/2/Lieut. A.A. BEER, reported for attachment as supernumary to Train from 15th. Divl. Train and is posted to No. 4 Company. Athy. A.S.C. (G.H.Q. 20312 dated 3/5/18. M.T. Coy. draw supplies from Railhead and dump at 29th. Divl. M.T. Coy's Camp - rations drawn to be kept there as reserve. No refilling to-day, but sufficient G.S. Wagons sent to Railhead to draw Sundries and Tobacco. Feeding strength 15,170.	
	12/5/18.		Railhead drawing by H.T. at 9 -0 a.m. Rations refilled and delivered after return of Company wagons from Railhead. Feeding strength 15,231.	
	13/5/18.		Showery. The following Units are added to the feeding strength of Division from to-day :- 119th. A.F.A. Bde., 19th. A.F.A. Bde., 28th. A.F.A.Bde., 64th. A.F.A. Bde. 87th. Brigade relieve 88th. Brigade on Left Sector od Divisional Front. Feeding Strength 17,706.	
	14/5/18.		Fine. T4/045067 Dr. Smith R.P., transferred to R.A.F., No.1 Aircraft Depot from 31/5/18.Athy. A.G's. A/7/55(02) dated 8-11-17. Feeding Strength 19,352.	
	15/5/18.		T/34861 Dr. Whr. Rowe, W.O., No. 4 Company evacuated to No. 2 C.C.S. Feeding Strength 19,136.	
	16/5/18.		S2/11699 Pte. W.E.L. Lavis appointed A/Cpl. vice. Cpl. Rosekelly with pay from 17/5/18 and effect from 31/10/17. xxxxxfxxxxxxfxxxx Athy. A.S.C. Section P21/8526/749 dated 6-5-18. 29th. Divl. Artillery draw from WARDRECQUES Railhead. Feeding Strength 20,907.	
	17/5/18.		Fine. The following reinforcements arrived from A.S.C. Base Depot and posted to No. 4 Coy :- T4/061993 Dr. Parker, J.F., T/313261 Dr. Andrews, J., T3/023597 Dr. Bragg, J.H., T4/123994 Dr Bailes, J. T3/023597 Dr. Bragg,J.H., transferred to 89th. Field Ambulance. S2/11699 A/Cpl. W.E.L. Lavis transferred from No. 2 Company to No. 4 Company. Feeding strength 21,315.	
	18/5/18.		T/37796 Dr. Carpenter,J.J., No.1 Company, evacuated to No. 2 C.C.S. 18/5/18. T4/061432 Dr. Smith H.W., No. 1 Company evacuated to C.C.S.,18/5/18. Feeding Strength 18,539.	
	19/5/18.		88th.Brigade relieve the 86th. Brigade in right sector of Divisional Front. Feeding Strength 18,067.	
	20/5/18.		Fine. T2/012097 Cpl. Holroyd evacuated to No. 2 C.C.S. T/37796 Dr. Carpenter discharged from No. 2 C.C.S. and taken on the strength. Feeding strength 17,865.	
	21/5/18.		Fine. Feeding strength 17,879.	

Army Form C. 2118.

WAR DIARY
or
INTELLIGENCE SUMMARY.   29th. Divisional Train.
(Erase heading not required.)

Place	Date	Hour	Summary of Events and Information	Remarks and references to Appendices
	22/5/18.		Capt.Sykes, R.A.M.C. attached to Divl. Train for duty. Feeding strength 17,925.	
	23/5/18.		Fine. 64th. A.F.A. Bde. draw for last time with this Division and wagons sent to report to No.4 Company, 1st. Australian Divisional Train. 1. H.D. horse evacuated by No.1 Coy: to 18th. M.V.S. 1 H.D. horse died of No. 4 Company. Feeding strength 17,847. 15 men of Brigade Coys inoculated.	
	24/5/18.		Wet. Railhead changed to EBBLINGHEM. 29th. Division draw at 8-30 a.m. No.1 Coys. refilling point moved to 27/U.19.a.8.8. 10 G.S. Wagons detailed to assist the evacuation of civilians from HAZEBROUCK. Feeding strength 16,935.	
	25/5/18.		Fine. S4/056702 Sgt. S.G.T. Rowe, M.M., No. 2 Company and T2/13478 C.S.M. A.C. Green, No. 2 Company evacuated to C.C.S. 25/5/18. Feeding strength 17,165.	
	26/5/18.		12 complete turnouts deducted from Special Establishment of Divisional Trains on account of the reduction of Infantry Brigades by one Battalion each. Athy. D.of T. No.15300/2 dated 23/5/18. Feeding Strength 15,750.	
	27/5/18.		Fine. Feeding Strength 16,032.	
	28/5/18.		The following reinforcements arrive from the Base and posted to Companys as follows :- T4/160532 Dr. Whr. Clarke,W.T. to No. 4 Coy., T/392000 Dr. Fitchie,T.T. to No.4 Coy. and S/383738 Pte. Webster,J.R. to No. 3 Company. S4/056713 Cpl. Shand proceeded to U.K. for Commission in the Infantry and struck off the strength of this Unit. Athy. No.62/79 dated 23/5/18. Feeding Strength 16,169.	
	29/5/18.		Fine. T4/043832 A/L/Cpl. Harbach,J. automatically reverted to permanent rank on being admitted to Hospital 9/5/18. Athy. Army Council Instructions 337 of 1917. Feeding strength 16,083.	
	30/5/18.		Capt. Malcom, R.A.M.C. attached to Divisional Train in relief of Captain Sykes, R.A.M.C. Feeding strength 15,974.	
	31/5/18.		1 G.S. Wagon detached from No. 2 Company to 196 Land Drainage Coy. Feeding strength 16,132.	

Lieut. Colonel, A.S.C.,
Commg., 29th. Divisional Train.

29th. DIVISIONAL TRAIN.

WAR DIARY,

for

the month of

June, 1918.

H.Q.,
29TH DIVL. TRAIN.
No.
Date.

Army Form C. 2118.

WAR DIARY
or
INTELLIGENCE SUMMARY.

29th. DIVISIONAL TRAIN.

(Erase heading not required.)

Instructions regarding War Diaries and Intelligence
Summaries are contained in F. S. Regs., Part II.
and the Staff Manual respectively. Title pages
will be prepared in manuscript.

Place	Date	Hour	Summary of Events and Information	Remarks and references to Appendices
WALLON CAPPEL	1/6/1918.		Leave reopens - 2 places allotted to the Train for the month of June. Feeding Strength:- 16,193	
	2/6/1918.		1 H.D. evacuated to 18th. M.V.S., from No.1 Company. Feeding Strength :- 16,216.	
	3/6/1918.		T/29198 A/Sgt. Hayden, F., evacuated to No. 2 C.C.S., from No. 4 Company. Lieut. Colonel E.T.L. Wright awarded D.S.O., Kings Birthday Honours. Feeding Strength :- 16,225.	
	4/6/1918.		87th. Brigade relieve the 88th. Brigade in the Line. T4/37301 Dr. Hodgson, H., No.1 Company, admitted to Field Ambulance 27/5/1918 and struck off the strength 4/6/1918	
	5/6/1918.		Captain D.P.C. Franks awarded the M.C., Captain J.S. Crone, Captain C.G. Taylor and T1/2846 Cpl. Tidby, T.H. mentioned in Despatches. The following reinforcements arrived from A.S.C., Base Depot. :- T/34861 Dr. Whr. Rowe, W.O., to No. 4 Coy., T4/263737 Dr. Jordan, C., to No.1 Coy. and T/387118 Dr. Holmes, W., to No.1 Coy. 1 mule evacuated from No. 3 Company to 18th. M.V.S. Feeding Strength :- 16,257.	
	6/6/1918.		TS/1017 Dr. Whr. Murphy. W., arrived from A.S.C. Base Depot and posted to No. 3 Company. Feeding Strength 16,296. 6 Limbered G.S. Wagons to report to 1st. Australian Division for special duty with "L" Special Company., R.E.	
	7/6/1918.		T4/37301 Dr. Hodgson, No.1 Coy., evacuated to C.C.S. T4/088721 Dr. Speer, G., No. 2 Company, appointed A/L/ Cpl., with pay from 8/6/18, and effect from 9/5/18. Athy. A.S.C.P.30/13637/8 dated 28/5/1918.	

Army Form C. 2118.

WAR DIARY
or
INTELLIGENCE SUMMARY.

(Erase heading not required.)

29th. DIVISIONAL TRAIN.

Instructions regarding War Diaries and Intelligence Summaries are contained in F. S. Regs., Part II. and the Staff Manual respectively. Title pages will be prepared in manuscript.

Place	Date	Hour	Summary of Events and Information	Remarks and references to Appendices
	7/6/1918.		T4/088721 A/L/Cpl. Speer, G. No.2 Company transferred to No. 4 Company. T4/32327 Dr. Gordon No. 4 Company, evacuated to No.2 C.C.S., and struck off the strength. Feeding Strength :- 16331.	
	8/6/1918.		T4/275214 Dr. Greaves, A., No.4 Company, evacuated to No.15 C.C.S. Feeding Strength :- 16,305.	
	9/6/1918.		Feeding Strength :- 16,307.	
	10/6/1918.		S/26558 S. Sgt. Taylor arrived from No. 3 Base Supply Depot, and posted to No.1 Company, but attached to No. 4 Company, vice S. Sgt. Cooper. Major F.H.A. Mayers granted Leave to U.K. from 10th./24th. June. Captain W.H. King, S.O., 87th. Brigade to act as Company Commander during his absence and 2nd/Lieut. Hollowell, No.1 Company to act as Supply Officer. 1 Rider evacuated from No. 4 Company to 18th. M.V.S. Feeding Strength :- 16,373. The French are anxious to obtain a record of all growing crops in the Forward Area, i.e., Area between the Front Line and the St. SYLVESTRE - HAZEBROUCK - MORBECQUE Road, with a view to attempts being made to harvest them in due course. 6 officers of the Train detailed to make a survey of this Area.	
Athy.	11/6/1918.		T4/037781 Sgt. Rogulski, A., No. 3 Company, transferred to R.A.F. and struck off the strength A.G. 2150/127 dated 5-6-1918. The 6 Limbered G.S. Wagons, with "L" Special Company, R.E. returned. Feeding Strength :- 16,870.	
	12/6/1918.		The following reinforcements arrived from A.S.C., Base Depot and taken on strength :-	

Army Form C. 2118.

WAR DIARY
or
INTELLIGENCE SUMMARY.

29th. DIVISIONAL TRAIN.

(Erase heading not required.)

Instructions regarding War Diaries and Intelligence Summaries are contained in F.S. Regs., Part II. and the Staff Manual respectively. Title pages will be prepared in manuscript.

Place	Date	Hour	Summary of Events and Information	Remarks and references to Appendices
			T/18749 A/C.S.M. H.C. House, to No. 2 Company, T/18749 A/C.S.M. H.C. House, to No. 2 Company, T4/142274 A/Sgt. Dorman, W.H., to No. 2 Company, T4/059748 Cpl. Manning, W. to No. 3 Company, T4/243841 Cpl. Kirby to No 4 Company, T4/124987 Dr. Dillon, F.C., No.1 Company, T4/343616 Dr. Dove, D. to 87th. Field Ambulance and T/392594 Dr. Cox, C.W. to No.2 Company. T/18528 C.Q.M.S. (A/S.S.M.) Mole, T., temporary promoted (D.of W.) to S.S.M., with effect from 11-9-17. Athy. A.S.C. P/30/13635/ dated 6-6-1918. T4/026836 Sgt. Rutland, J.W., evacuated to No. 2 C.C.S. Feeding Strength 16,770.	
	13/6/1918.		On the night of the 12th./13th. the 88th. Infantry Brigade relieved by the 86th. Infantry Bde., in the Left Sector of the Divisional Front. Feeding Strength :- 17,728.	
	14/6/1918.		Feeding Strength :- 17,426.	
	15/6/1918.		Feeding Strength :- 17,272. 1 mule, No. 3 Company, died (ruptured intestines) T1/090416 A/Cpl. Cummings, R., No.1 Company, admitted to 88th. Field Ambulance.	
	16/6/1918.		Feeding Strength :- 16,729.	
	17/6/1918.		1. H.D. horse evacuated to 18th. M.V.S., from No.1 Company. Feeding Strength :- 17,056.	
	18/6/1918.		Survey of crops in Forward Area completed. T4/122172 Dr. Warren, C.E.J., admitted to 88th. Field Ambulance, from No.1 Company. 1 H.D. Horse evacuated to 18th. M.V.S., from No.1 Company T4/088570 Dr. Anderson, J. and T/313261 Dr. Andrews, J., admitted to 88th. Field Ambulance. Feeding Strength :- 17,273.	

Army Form C. 2118.

WAR DIARY
or
INTELLIGENCE SUMMARY.

29th. DIVISIONAL TRAIN.

(Erase heading not required.)

Instructions regarding War Diaries and Intelligence
Summaries are contained in F. S. Regs., Part II.
and the Staff Manual respectively. Title pages
will be prepared in manuscript.

Place	Date	Hour	Summary of Events and Information	Remarks and references to Appendices
	19/6/1918.		Warning Order received that the Division is being relieved by the 31st. Division, on nights 20th./21st. and 21st./22nd. Artillery in Offensive positions to return to defensive positions Division to be in Army reserve. T4/088570 Dr. Anderson, J. and T/313261 Dr. Andrews, J., No. 4 Company, evacuated to No. 2 C.C.S. T4/122172 Dr. Warren, C.E.J., evacuated to No.2 C.C.S., from No.1 Company. T4/108144 Cpl. Colgate, W.A., No.4 Company, evacuated to No. 4 C.C.S. 1 Rider evacuated to 18th. M.V.S., from No. 2 Company.	
	20/6/1918.		No. 4 Company move to LUMBRES Area, staging the night 20th/21st. in WIZERNES. 1 Rider from S.A.A., Section, and posted to No. 4 Company. Feeding Strength :- 16,824.	
	21/6/1918.		M.T. draw for 88th. Brigade Group from EBBLINGHEM Railhead and dump at LUMBRES. T4/090416 A/Cpl. Cummings, R., No.1 Company, discharged from Hospital. Feeding Strength :- 16,577.	
	22/6/1918.		T.H.Q. move from WALLON CAPPEL to WARDRECQUES. No.3 Company move to Camp at 36A/B.8.b.0.6. Draw for the last time from EBBLINGHEM Railhead.	
WARDREC-QUES.	23/6/1918.		The following reinforcements arrived from A.S.C., Base Depot, and posted to Nos. 4 and 1 Coys, respectively :- T2/10920 Sgt. Flowerday, S.T. and T4/238258 Dr. Hattam, J.W. S4/064456 A/Cpl. Sands, G.S. promoted to substantive rank of Cpl., with effect from 9-10-17. Athy. A.S.C. P/21/8526/749 dated 21-6-1918. Orders received that 86th. Brigade will move on the 24th. to	

Army Form C. 2118.

WAR DIARY
or
INTELLIGENCE SUMMARY.

29th. DIVISIONAL TRAIN.

(Erase heading not required.)

Instructions regarding War Diaries and Intelligence Summaries are contained in F.S. Regs., Part II. and the Staff Manual respectively. Title pages will be prepared in manuscript.

Place	Date	Hour	Summary of Events and Information	Remarks and references to Appendices
BLARINGHEM AREA.	24/6/1918.		Draw from WARDRECQUES Railhead to-day, except No 4 Group who draw from LOMBRES Railhead. Feeding Strength :- 15,940. T2/018097 Cpl. Holroyd, W.H., from A.S.C., Base Depot and posted to No. 4 Company. No.2 Company move to Camp at 36A/B.12.b.5.3. Major F.H.A. Mayers returned from leave and resumed duties as O.C. No. 3 Company.	
	25/6/1918.		T4/088570 Dr. Anderson, J., rejoined from Hospital and posted to No. 4 Company. 1 Battalion of the 86th. Brigade remain in Forward Area and are rationed by 31st. Division. T2/10107 Dr. Holder, F., No. 4 Company, evacuated to 18th. C.C.S. Feeding Strength :-16,051.	
	26/6/1918.		T4/106144 Cpl. Colgate, discharged from Hospital and posted to No. 4 Company. Feeding Strength 14,716.	
	27/6/1918.		T4/036948 A/Whr. Cpl. Mitchell, H.E., promoted to substantive rank, with effect from 11/11/17, within original establishment, Athy. A.S.C. P21/8526/7/49 dated 24/6/1918. T4/043855 Whr.S.Sgt. Blackburn, W., granted 3d. per day, additional pay, with effect from 20/5/18. Authority A.S.C./20293/345 dated 24-6-1918. T2/13478 C.S.M. Green, A.C. rejoined from Base and posted to No. 2 Company. Feeding Strength :- 14,597.	
	28/6/1918.		T/313261 Dr. Andrews, J., rejoined from Hospital and posted to No. 4 Company. Feeding Strength:- 15,231.	

Army Form C. 2118.

WAR DIARY
or
INTELLIGENCE SUMMARY.

29th. DIVISIONAL TRAIN.

(Erase heading not required.)

Place	Date	Hour	Summary of Events and Information	Remarks and references to Appendices
	29/6/1918.		1 Rider and 1 H.D., No.2 Company, evacuated to 18th. M.V.S. Feeding Strength :- 15,658.	
	30/6/1918.		No. 2 Company, move to new camp at 36A/A.18.d. central. Feeding strength 16,060. The following N.C.Os., awarded the M.S.M., King's Birthday Honour List, (extracts from London Gazette, 15th. to 20th. June, 1918) TS/9943 Farr. S. Sgt. Wakely, G.F., S4/056614 S.Sgt. Stevens, F.E., T4/043889 Sgt. Pearce, S4/056879 Sgt. Sandiford, P.	

Lieut. Colonel, A.S.C.,

Commg., 29th. Divisional Train.

29th. DIVISIONAL TRAIN.

WAR DIARY
for
July, 1918.

Army Form C. 2118.

WAR DIARY
or
INTELLIGENCE SUMMARY.

29th. Divisional Train.

(Erase heading not required.)

Instructions regarding War Diaries and Intelligence Summaries are contained in F. S. Regs. Part II. and the Staff Manual respectively. Title pages will be prepared in manuscript.

Place	Date	Hour	Summary of Events and Information	Remarks and references to Appendices
WARDREC-QUES.	1/7/1918.		T4/056973 Dr. Kehoe, P. No.1 Company, evacuated to C.C.S., on 27th June. T4/122172 Dr. Warren, G.E.J. rejoined from C.C.S. 2 H.D. from 18th. M.V.S. and posted to No.1 Company. Feeding strength 15,462.	
	2/7/1918.		T4/240726 Dr. Vickery, No.4 Coy., rejoined from Hospital. 2/Lieut. J.S. Bracegirdle, granted 14 days leave to the U.K. Feeding Strength :- 15,647.	
	3/7/1918. 4/7/1918		Feeding Strength :- 15,628. T/27455 A/Cpl. Squires, F.T., from A.S.C., Base Depot and posted to No.1 Company. Feeding Strength :- 15,308.	
	5/7/1918. 6/7/1918.		Feeding Strength :- 15,530. T4/151351 Dr. Rumble, No. 3 Company, admitted to 89th. Field Ambulance. T1/2846 Cpl. T.H. Tidby, rejoined from A.S.C. Base Depot and posted to No.4 Company. Feeding Strength :- 15,420.	
	7/7/1918.		T4/199726 Dr. Sadd. Bishley, No.1 Company, admitted to 87th. Field Ambulance. Feeding Strength :- 13,445.	
	8/8/1918. 9/7/1918.		Feeding Strength :- 13,452. T4/243941 Cpl. Kirby,F.W., No.4 Company admitted to 88th. Field Ambulance. Feeding Strength :- 14,043.	
	10/7/1918. 11/7/1918. 12/7/1918.		Lieut. W.E.C. Hulme, granted leave to the U.K. for 14 days. Feeding Strength :- 14,695. Feeding Strength :- 14,640. 1st. Border Regt, of 87th. Infty. Bde. move to 27/V.15.d. and come under the administration of 1st. Australian Division. T/18749 A/C.S.M. House, H.C. to A.S.C. Base Depot, Surplus to Establishment. The following remounts are drawn from 18th. M.V.S.:- 2 L.D. and 5 H.D. animals. Notification received that Capt. (T/Major) F.H.A. Mayers, A.S.C., (S.R.) should proceed to U.K. Authority A.S.C. 20849 dated 9-7-1918. Feeding Strength :- 14,596.	
	13/7/1918.		Orders received that the 87th. Bde., 1 Coy., of 29th. Bn. M.G.Corps and 1 Company of the Train will move to the 1st. Australian Divisional Area. One Infantry Bde. of the 1st. Australian Division, 1 Coy. of 1st. ANX Bn. Aus: M.G. Corps and 1 Train Company will move to 29th. Divl: Area. Rations for the 1st. Border Regiment taken to them by lorry. Feeding Strength :- 14,629.	
	14/7/1918.		No. 3 Company, move to Camp at 27/U.17.c.8.9. and come under the administration of 1st. Aus: Div: No. 3 Group draw for the last time from our park at EBBLINGHEM Railhead. T3/026318 Dr. Hogarth, R. No. 2 Company evacuated to No. 2 Australian C.C.S. Location of No. 2 Groups Refilling Point now POINT ASQUIN. Capt.(T/Major) F.H.A. Mayers, proceed to U.K. Command of No. 3 Company taken over by T/ Capt.W.H.King, S.O. 87th. Infty. Bde., and Supply Duties to be performed by T/2nd. Lieut. T. Dwane. T4/199736 Dr. Sadd. Bishley,E.T., No.1 Company,	

Army Form C. 2118.

WAR DIARY
or
INTELLIGENCE SUMMARY. 29th. Divisional Train.

(Erase heading not required.)

Place	Date	Hour	Summary of Events and Information	Remarks and references to Appendices
	15/7/1918.		admitted to 88th. Field Ambulance, 6/7/1918 and struck off the strength as from to-day. 1 H.D. Horse, No. 2 Company evacuated to 18th. M.V.S. Feeding Strength :- 13,214. T/392877 Dr. Far. Mc.Leod, J. from A.S.C. Base Depot and posted to No. 2 Company. T4/090416 A/Cpl. Cummings, R., No.1 Comapny and T2/018097 Cpl. Holroyd, W.H., No. 4 Comapny to A.S.C. Base Depot, Surplus to Establishment. T4/243941 Cpl. Kirby, F.W.,No. 4 Company, evacuated to 17th. C.C.S. T2/10920 Sgt. Flowerday, S.J., No. 4 Company, admitted to 88th. Field Ambulance. Feeding Strength :- 14,836.	
	16/7/1918.		Six men of the Train proceed to Second Army Rest Camp at AUDRESSELLES for aperiod of 14 days. T4/039067 C.Q.M.S. Smith, A.H., No. 3 Company, granted increase of pay at 3d.per day, as from 26/2/1918. Authority A.S.C./20293/395 dated 12-7-1918. Feeding Strength :- 15,034.	
	17/7/1918.		1 H.D. Horse from 18th. M.V.S. to No. 2 Company. Feeding Strength :- 15,050.	
	18/7/1918.		2 N.C.Os of the Train sent to XV Corps School for a course of Hotchkiss Gun Instruction. 1 H.D. Horse, No. 3 Company, evacuated to 41st. M.V.S. Feeding Strength :- 15,786.	
	19/7/1918.		88th. Bde move from LUMBRES Area and draw from our pack to-day. No. 4 Company Camp at 27/t.27.d.9.9. 87th. Bde. concentrate in the BLARINGHEM Area, except one Company of the 29th. Bn. M.G. Corps. No. 3 Company Camp at 36A/B.16. b.4.0. Feeding Strength :- 17,698.	
	20/7/1918.		Feeding Strength :- 17,755.	
	21/7/1918.		The following reinforcements arrive from A.S.C. Base Depot:- T/420311 Dr. Bamford,M., T/185387 Blayney, D., T/313358 Dr. Bysouth, G. to No.1 Company, T/370968 Dr. Macreavie, T., to No. 2 Company, T4/174299 Dr. Bing, A., T4/246533 Dr. Beetlestone, G.E., to No. 4 Company and T/418566 Dr. Parker, T., to 88th. Field Ambulance. Feeding Strength :- 17,058.	
	22/7/1918.		T2/210920 Sgt. Flowerday, S.J., No. 4 Company, struck off the strength, admitted to 88th. Field Ambulance, 15/7/1918. 1 H.D. Horse evacuated to Corps Evacuation Hospital from No. 2 Coy. Division move from WARDRECQUES AREA to CASSEL AREA, No.1 Company Camp at 27/N.21.a.9.4., No.2 Company, N.6.d.0.5., No. 3 Company P.20.c.7.8., No.4 Company O.16.b.5.9., Train Headquarters at BAVINCHOVE. Feeding Strength :- 18,864	
	23/7/1918.		T/23731 Dr. Abrams, J., transferred to A.S.C. Base Depot, Surplus to Establishment. Feeding Strength :- 18,497.	
	24/7/1918.		T2/10920 Sgt. Flowerday, S.J., No. 4 Company from Hospital and returned to No. 4 Company. T4/199736 Dr. Bishley, E.T., from Hospital and returned to No.1 Company. Feeding Strength :- 15,470. Railhead changes to CASSEL.	
	25/7/1918.		1/2 Mons Regt., 2/Hants. Regt., 455th. Field Company, R.E., and 510th. Field Company, R.E., move to Forward Area. Supply Dump opened in their vicinity. Feeding Strength :- 15,598.	
	26/7/1918.		T4/042387 Sad. Cpl. Gregory, A. transferred from No. 3 Company to No. 1 Company. T4/124244 Sad.	

Army Form C. 2118.

WAR DIARY
or
INTELLIGENCE SUMMARY. 29th. Divisional Train.
(Erase heading not required.)

Instructions regarding War Diaries and Intelligence Summaries are contained in F.S. Regs., Part II. and the Staff Manual respectively. Title pages will be prepared in manuscript.

Place	Date	Hour	Summary of Events and Information	Remarks and references to Appendices
	27/7/1918.		Cpl. Hartman, W., transferred from No. 1 Company to No. 3 Company. Feeding Strength :- 15,153.	
	28/7/1918.		Feeding Strength :- 15,865. T4/243941 Cpl. Kirby, F.W., from 17th. C.C.S., and returned to No. 4 Company. Feeding Strength :- 15,652.	
	29/7/1918.		Feeding Strength :- 15,584.	
	30/7/1918.		T4/239072 A/Sgt. Church, from A.S.C. Base Depot and posted to No.1 Company. Feeding Strength :- 15,945.	
	31/7/1918.		Warning Order received re Division relieving 1st. Australian Division in STRAZEELE Sector of the XV Corps Front on 1st., 2nd. and 3rd. August. Feeding Strength :- 16,993.	

Lieut. Colonel, A.S.C.,
Commg., 29th. Divisional Train.

Army Form C. 2118.

WAR DIARY
or
INTELLIGENCE SUMMARY
(Erase heading not required.)

29th. Divisional Train.

Instructions regarding War Diaries and Intelligence Summaries are contained in F.S. Regs., Part II. and the Staff Manual respectively. Title pages will be prepared in manuscript.

Place	Date	Hour	Summary of Events and Information	Remarks and references to Appendices
BAVINCHOVE	1/8/1918.		Feeding Strength :- 15,657.	
	2/8/1918.		Nos. 1, 2 and 4 Coys move to New Area, camps as follows :- No.1 Coy. 27/U.18.Cent.: No 2 Coy. U.18.a.1.9. No.4 Coy.U.17.6.4.7. Last day of drawing from BAVINCHOVE Railhead. T.Captain A.S. Lee, joined from 36th. Divl: and posted to No.3 Company, as supply officer. T3/031393 Dr.Bond, H., from 36th. Divl: Train and posted to No.3 Company. Feeding Strength :- 15,620.	
	3/8/1918.		Train Headquarters move to New Area and camp at U.18.b.3.5. No 3 Company move to Camp at U.19.c.9.8. Railhead changed to EBBLINGHEM. Feeding strength :- 18,623.	
	4/8/1918.		T2/10699 Dr. Johns, J., No.1 Coy: admitted to 87th. XXX Field Ambulance. TS/8962 Saddler Wigglesworth, H., from A.S.C. Base Depot and posted to No.1 Coy. Feeding Strength :- 18,435.	
	5/8/1918.		Feeding Strength :- 18,849.	
	6/8/1918.		T4/160961 Capl. Hall, E., No.1 Company, proceeded to U.K. as candidate for T. Commission in the Infantry and struck off the strength. Feeding Strength :- 17,284.	
	7/8/1918.		T/392877 Farr. Dr. McLeod to A.S.C. Base Depot, Surplus to Establishment from No. 2 Coy: The undermentioned Category "B" Drivers arrive from A.S.C. Base Depot to replace 10 Category "A" Drivers, who have to be sent to the Base for transfer to the Infantry :- T/292051 Dr. Crookbain, G.E., T/236190 Dr. Bloomfield, H., T/356842 Dr Brassington, H., T/386488 Dr.Harper, P. to No. 1 Coy: T4/144230 Dr.Crate, W.; T2364375 Dr. Currie, L, to No. 2 Company: T/313318 Dr. Cockhill, A.J., T/370598 Dr. Curren, T., to No. 3 Coy : T/370294 Dr. Chattaway, W., T/370441 Dr. Crouch, W., to No.4 Coy. Authority D.A.G., GR.32001/2 dated 30-7-1918. Feeding Strength :- 17,394.	
	8/8/1918.		The following Category "A" Drivers sent to A.S.C. Base Depot for transfer to the Infantry :- T4/161147 Dr. Baldwin, J., T4/160443 Dr. T.R. Bush, T4/143735 T. Dilkes, T3/16095 Dr.Maynard,T.G. from No.1 Coy : T4/038208 Dr. Futter, F.J.H., T4/044093 Dr. S.Parkes from No.2 Coy : T4/043729 Dr. Richards, H., T3/026668 Dr.Mutch, E., from No. 3 Coy : T3/023757 Dr. McGee, R., T4/124232 Dr. Nield, W., from No.4 Coy. T/370598 Dr. Curren transferred from No. 3 Coy. to No.1 Coy to complete the latters establishment. Major W.G. Marchbanks, (T.F.) from A.S.C. Base Depot and posted to No.1 Company. Athy: ST(P) 1551/634 dated 4/8/1918. Feeding Strength :- 16,907.	
	9/8/1918.		Feeding Strength :- 17, 278.	
	10/8/1918.		S4/060487 A/Cpl. Ludgate, H.C.W., from A.S.C. Base depot and posted to No.1 Company. T2/15384 Dr. Gerrish, H., from 88th. Brigade H.Q., to No.4 Coy and T/364914 Dr. Dalton, W., from No. 4 Company to 88th. Brigade H.Q. Feeding Strength :- 17,426.	
	11/8/1918.		Feeding Strength :- 17,167.	

Army Form C. 2118.

WAR DIARY
or
INTELLIGENCE SUMMARY.

29th. Divisional Train.

(Erase heading not required.)

Instructions regarding War Diaries and Intelligence Summaries are contained in F.S. Regs., Part II. and the Staff Manual respectively. Title pages will be prepared in manuscript.

Place	Date	Hour	Summary of Events and Information	Remarks and references to Appendices
	12/8/1918.		T2/10699 Dr. Johns, J.H., No.1 Coy: admitted to 87th. Field Ambulance 4/8/1918, struck off the strength 12/8/1918. 1 G.S. Wagons complete turnout, from Base, for 29th. Bn. M.G. Corps, and taken on the strength of No.1 Company. T/291223 Dr. Priestly, E., from Base and posted to No.1 Coy. Feeding Strength :- 16,992.	
	13/8/1918.		Feeding Strength :- 17,036.	
	14/8/1918.		T.Capt. W.H. King, granted leave to U.K. from 14th. to 28th. Aug., 1918. T.Capt. A.S. Lee to command No.3 Company during Capt. King's absence. Feeding Strength :- 17,065.	
	15/8/1918.		T4/160562 Dr. Whr. Clarke, A.J., No.4 Coy: admitted to 88th. Field Ambulance Feeding Strength :- 17,262.	
	16/8/1918.		T4/042455 A/Cpl. Jennings, T., No.2 Coy: promoted Cpl.effect from 20-11-15 and T4/042614 A/Cpl. Stephens, R.J., No.3 Coy: promoted Cpl. effect from 10-6-1915. Athy: A.S.C. P/21/ 8526/749 dated 2-8-1918. Feeding Strength :- 16,871.	
	17/8/1918.		T4/243941 Cpl.Kirby, T.W, No.4 Coy: transferred to No.1 Company. Feeding Strength :- 17,147.	
	18/8/1918.		The following Drivers arrive from A.S.C. Base Depot and posted to 89th. Field Ambulance :- T4/126344 Dr. Byfield, A.; T/421701 Dr. Beaumont,A.;T/420330 Dr. Bailey, J.; T/42275 Dr. Belcher, J.H.; from Base and posted to 88th. Field Ambulance. T/421892 Dr. Broad, J.H. from Base and posted to No. 2 Coy: T/364375 Dr. Currie, J., transferred from No. 2Coy. to 89th. Field Ambulance. Feeding Strength :- 16,666.	
	19/8/1918.		T.2nd. Lieut. J.C. Thorold, transferred from No. 4 Coy. to No. 3 Coy. T4/160562 Dr. Whr. Clarke, A.J., evacuated to 64th. C.C.S. Feeding Strength :- 16,718.	
	20/8/1918		T4/042387 Sadd. Cpl. Gregory, A., No.1 Company, evacuated. T.2nd. Lieut. S.S. Lockwood, No. 3 Coy. transferred to 50th. Divl: Train Athy. S.T.P. 1531/659 dated 14-8-1918. Feeding Strength:- 16,933.	
	21/8/1918.		T4/199736 Dr. Sadd. Bishley, E.T. to A.S.C. Base Depot, from No.1 Coy. Surplus to Establishment. Feeding Strength :- 16,842.	
	22/8/1918.		1 H.D. Animal, No. 2 Company, evacuated to 18th.M.V.S. Feeding Strength :- 17,288	
	23/8/1918.		T.2nd. Lieut. J.H. Hollowell, transferred from No.1 Coy to No. 3 Coy. T.2nd. Lieut. T. Dwane, No. 3 Coy. transferred to 57th. Divl: Train Athy. 29th. Div. No. 979 dated 22/8/1918. Feeding Strength :- 16,476.	
	24/8/1918.		Lieut. H. Harris, No. 4 Coy: granted Special Leave to U.K. from 24th.Aug., to 7/9/1918. Athy: XV.Corps A.C.L. 2922 dated 22/8/1918. 1 H.D. Animal from 18th. M.V.S. to No. 2 Coy. Feeding Strength :- 15,614.	

Army Form C. 2118.

WAR DIARY

or
INTELLIGENCE SUMMARY

(Erase heading not required.)

29th. Divisional Train.

Place	Date	Hour	Summary of Events and Information	Remarks and references to Appendices
	25/8/1918.		T. Lieuts. L.C. Shadwell and W.E.C. Hulme promoted A/Captains whilst employed with Divl: Trains dated 2nd. Aug.,1918. Extracts from List No. 201 Appointments, Commissions, etc., dated 18th. Aug., 1918. Feeding Strength :- 16,821.	
	26/8/1918.		S/312220 Pte. Lockton, J.G. No. 4 Coy. transferred to A.S.C. Base Depot. Athy: A.S.C. Section Circular No. 86 dated 21-8-1918. Feeding Strength :- 16,169.	
	27/8/1918.		Feeding Strength :- 16,729.	
	28/8/1918.		S4/060489 A/Cpl. Ludgate, H.C. admitted to 88th. Field Ambulance. TS/7646 Dr. Whr. Vipond,H., from 9th. Divl: Train and posted to No. 4 Coy. Feeding Strength :- 17,307.	
	29/8/1918.		T4/23550 Dr. Pickering, G., from 41st. Divisional Train and posted to 88th. Field Ambulance Divisional Headquarters move to BORRE from ST. SYLVESTRE CAPPEL. Feeding Strength :- 16,561. Feeding Strength :- 16,701.	
	30/8/1918. 1/8/1918.		Divisional Train move forward as units are now too far away owing to Advance. Train H.Q., at BORRE, No.1 Coy. at V.24.b.4.4. No. 2 Coy. W.23.c.9.8. No. 3 Coy. W.21.a.6.9. No. 4 Coy. W.21.b.7.0. (All sheet 27). Feeding Strength :- 17,233.	

Geo Marchant Major
for Lieut. Colonel, A.S.C.,
Commg., 29th. Divisional Train.

Army Form C. 2118.

WAR DIARY
or
~~INTELLIGENCE SUMMARY~~ 29th. Divisional Train.
(Erase heading not required.)

Instructions regarding War Diaries and Intelligence Summaries are contained in F.S. Regs., Part II. and the Staff Manual respectively. Title pages will be prepared in manuscript.

Place	Date	Hour	Summary of Events and Information	Remarks and references to Appendices
BORRE.	1-9-18.		Feeding Strength:- 16,721.	
"	2-9-18.		Feeding Strength:- 17,051. T4/056997, Dr.Smith, O. No. 2 Coy. Admitted Div. Rest Station.	
"	3-9-18.		Feeding Strength:- 18,206. T4/056602, Dr.Weeks,E. transferred from No. 1 Coy. to No. 3 Coy. and T4/088314, Dr. Copping, S. transferred from No. 3 Coy. to No. 1 Coy. Railhead changes to HAZEBROUCK.	
"	4-9-18.		~~XXXXXXXXX~~ Feeding Strength:-17,885. S4/060489, a/Cpl.Ludgate, H.C. No.1 Coy.discharged from Hosp.	
"	5-9-18.		Feeding Strength:- 16,363. T4/056997 Dr. Smith, O. No. 2 Coy. discharged from Div. Rest Station.	
"	6-9-18.		Feeding Strength:- 17,516. Lt.Col. E.T.L. Wright granted leave to U.K. from 6-9-18 to 20-9-18. Major Marchbank to command the Train during his absence. Nos. 1 and 3 Coys. move their camps to 36/A 4 c 7.5 and /X 21 c 9.9 respectively.	
"	7-9-18.		Feeding Strength:- 20,101. The 31st. Division relieves the 29th. Division, the latter assembling in the BAILLEUL-METEREN area. 4 Riders and 1 H.D. animals drawn from 18th. Mob. Vet. Section.	
"	8-9-18.		Feeding Strength:- 17,865. Capt. R2C.O. Viveash granted 14 days leave to U.K. from 8-9-18 to 22-9-18. 2Lt. J.H. Hollowell to act as Supply Officer, 86th. Brigade during his absence. Railhead changes to BAILLEUL. T/Capt. R.W.H. Hedger, from 3rd. Cavalry Reserve Park and posted to No. 1 Coy. Authy. XV Corps wire No. A.M.6 of 6th.inst. T4/242707, Sadd.Cpl. Warr, H.T.J. from A.S.C. Base Depot, and posted to No. 1 Coy. T4/160189, Dr. Wood, H. from 3rd. Cavalry Reserve Park and posted to No. 1 Coy.	
"	9-9-18.		Feeding Strength:- 16,657. ~~XXXXXXXXXXXXXXXXXXXXXXXXXXXXXXXXXXX~~ Railhead changes to CAESTRE.	
"	10-9-18.		Feeding Strength:- 17,404. Railhead changes to BAILLEUL.	
"	11-9-18.		Feeding Strength:- 17,323. 29th. Div. Artillery moving to Fletre area on night 12/13th inst. 87th. Brigade moving to Wallon Cappel area on 12th. inst. Railhead changes to HAZEBROUCK GARAGE. The 86th. and 88th. Infantry Brigades move to Hazebrouck-Hondeghem area. No. 2 Coy. moves to camp at V 22 c ~~XXX~~ 35.70 and No. 4 Coy. moves to camp at V 16 c 3.9. M.T. draw supplies from Railhead.	
"	12-9-18.		Feeding Strength:- 18,049. No. 3 Coy. moves to new area and camp at ST. JAN TER BIEZEN. No. 1 Coy. move to new camp at W 18 d 1.5. Supplies for No. 1 and 3 Coys. drawn from Railhead by M.T. No. 2 and 4 Coys. draw by H.T.	
"	13-9-18.		Feeding Strength:- 14,029. T/2nd Lt. A. Forbes, No. 4 Coy., granted leave to U.K. from 13-9-18 to 27-9-18. T/2nd Lt. W.E. Balmer will act as S.O. during his absence.	
"	14-9-18.		Feeding Strength:- 20,807. 29th. Div. Artillery move to DROGLANDT area on night of 15/15th. No. 1	
"	15-9-18.		Feeding Strength:- 14,501. Coy. camp on the night of the 15th. at 27/J 12 b 8.7. M.T. dump supplies drawn for No. 1 Group at No. 1 Coy's camp. T/18819, C.S.M. Stephens, No. 3 Coy. admitted 87th. Field Ambulance. S4/056850, Cpl. Gomm, No. 3 Coy. admitted 87th. Field Ambulance. 1 mule trans. from 4 to 3 Coy.	

Army Form C. 2118.

WAR DIARY
or
INTELLIGENCE SUMMARY

(Erase heading not required.)

29th. Divisional Train.

Instructions regarding War Diaries and Intelligence Summaries are contained in F.S. Regs., Part II. and the Staff Manual respectively. Title pages will be prepared in manuscript.

Place	Date	Hour	Summary of Events and Information	Remarks and references to Appendices
	16-9-18.		Feeding Strength :- 14,040. T2nd. Lieut. F.N. Creer, No.1 Company, granted leave to the U.K. from 16-9-18 to 30-9-1918. T. Capt. O. Blount to act as supply officer during his absence. The 87th. Infty. Bde. move to New Area, No.3 Company move to Camp at 27/F.25.b.3.9. I.H.D. animal evacuated to 18th. M.V.S. by No.4 Company. T. Capt. W.E.C. Hulme, transferred from No.2 Company to No.4 Company, and assumed command of that Company from T. Lieut. H.Harris. T. 2nd. Lieut. J.S. Bracegirdle, No.1 Comapny transferred to No.2 Comapny.	
	17-9-18.		Feeding Strength :- 14,188. T.H.Q. move from BORRE to VOGELTJE CONVENT, F.22.cent. M.T. draw from Railhead for all Companies.	
	18-9-18.		Feeding Strength :- 14,629. 87th. Infty. Bde. and one Company 29th. Bn. M.G. Corps ordered to move forward to take over part of YPRES Front on night 19th./20th. 86th. Infty. Bde. move from HAZEBROUCK Area to YPR S Area on night 19th./20th.	
	19-9-18.		Feeding Strength :- 14,550. Nos.2 and 3 Companies move to Camps at 28/A.14.b.6.4.	
	20-9-18.		T/18819 C.S.M. Stevens, No. 3 Company from Divl. Rest Station. Feeding Strength + 14,489.	
	21-9-18.		Feeding Strength :- 15,760. Railhead changes to INTERNATIONAL CORNER. Nos. 2 and 3 Companies draw by H.T. from Railhead. No. 4 Company move from Camp at HAZEBROUCK to Camp at 27/F.25.b. 3.9. Nos. 2 and 3 Companies move to Camp at 28/A.20.b.6.4. which is under construction. S4/056850 Cpl. Gomm, No. 3 Company, from Divl. Rest Station.	
	22-9-18.		Feeding Strength :- 15,992. No.1 Company move to Camp at 28/A. 3.a.1.0. Notification received to sent to Reinforcements ROUEN. T.13291 A/C.S.M. Grayburn, G., for A.S.C. Malarial Units. Authority:- A.S.C. Section Wire S.B. 300 dated 21-9-1918. T4/143735 Dr. Dilkes, from A.S.C. Base Depot and posted to No.1 Company. T. Capt. C.G. Taylor No. 2 Company, granted leave to the U.K. from 22/9/18 to 6/10/1918.	
	23-9-18.		Feeding Strength :- 15, 943. H.T. draw supplies from Railhead for Nos. 1, 2 and 3 Companies. No.4 Company still drawing by M.T. T/13291 A/C.S.M. Grayburn, G., No.1 Company, proceeded to Reinforcements, ROUEN. T/259987 Dr. Chambers, T., No.1 Company, transferred to 89th. Field Ambulance.	
	24-9-18.		Feeding Strength :- 16,451. T. Capt. O. Blount, No.1 Company, transferred to 3rd. Cavalry Reserve Park. Authority. XV. Corps Wire No. A.M.6 dated 6-9-1918. No.3 Company move to 28/F.25.b.3.9. and No. 4 Company to 28/A.20.b.6.4. T4/146797 Dr. Organ, N.A., No.1 Company, transferred to 3rd. Cavalry Reserve Park. No. 3 Coy. move to F/37 b 3.9. and No. 4 Coy. to 28/A 20 b 6.4.	
	25-9-18.		Feeding Strength:- 16,300.	
	26-9-18.		Feeding Strength:- 16,188.	
	27-9-18.		Feeding Strength:- 16,011. 2Lt. A.A.Beer No. 4 Coy. granted leave to U.K. from 27-9-18 to 11-10-18. Div. H.Q. and Train move from VOGELTJE Convent to BRAKE CAMP.	

Army Form C. 2118.

WAR DIARY
or
INTELLIGENCE SUMMARY

29tht Divisional Train.

(Erase heading not required.)

Instructions regarding War Diaries and Intelligence Summaries are contained in F. S. Regs., Part II. and the Staff Manual respectively. Title pages will be prepared in manuscript.

Place	Date	Hour	Summary of Events and Information	Remarks and references to Appendices
	28-9-18.		Feeding Strength:- 16,522. Owing to Infantry advance, all Coys. move up and camp out during the night. Major W.G. Marchbank wounded in left foot by shell, and evacuated to No. 2 Can.C.C.S. T/2nd. Lt. A.A. Beer attached to No. 4 Coy. transferred to No. 1 Coy.	
	29-9-18.		Feeding Strength:- 17,380.	
	30-9-18.		Feeding Strength:- 16,222. Railhead changes to VLAMERTINGHE.	

Lieut. Colonel, A.S.C.,
Comm g., 29th. Divisional Train.

Army Form C. 2118.

WAR DIARY
or
INTELLIGENCE SUMMARY.
(Erase heading not required.)

29th. Divisional Train.

Instructions regarding War Diaries and Intelligence Summaries are contained in F.S. Regs. Part II. and the Staff Manual respectively. Title pages will be prepared in manuscript.

Place	Date	Hour	Summary of Events and Information	Remarks and references to Appendices
BRAKE CAMP	1/10/18.		Feeding Strength, 16,835. T4/035771 A/S.S.M. Pollard, E., and T4/126524 Sad.S.Sgt. George, A.E. No.2 Company, admitted to 29th Divisional Rest Station. 1 H.D. Animal, No.3 Company destroyed by Vet. Officer.	
	2/10/1918		Feeding Strength :- 16,343. T.Capt. R.W.A. Hedger, No.1 Company granted leave to the U.K. from 2-10-18 to 16-10-1918.	
	3/10/18.		Feeding Strength :- 16,162. The following N.C.Os. promoted to substantive rank, authority A.S.C. P43/16836 dated 23-9-18:- T4/239072 A/Sgt. Church,F.W. No.1 Coy., to be Sgt. d/- 29-7-1918, T4/250897 A/Far. Cpl. Reynard, W.G., No.1 Coy., to Far. Cpl. d/- 10-3-18, S4/060489 A/Cpl. Ludgate, H.C.W. No.1 Company to be Cpl. d/- 10-8-18, S2/11699 A/Cpl. Lavis, W.E.L. No.4 Coy., to be Cpl. d/- 31-10-17, T4/036963 A/L/Cpl. Beulah, R., No.4 Coy., to L/Cpl. d/- 2-2-1916. 1 L.D. animal, No.3 Company, killed by shell fire.	
	4-10-18.		Feeding Strength :- 15,901. Captain & Adjutant C.E. Browne, M.C., granted leave to the U.K. from 4th.-10-18 to 18-10-18. T2nd. Lieut. W.J.C. Thorold, No.3 Company, to act as Adjutant during his absence. T4/035771, A/S.S.M. Pollard E. and T4/126524 Sad. S. Sgt. George, A.E., No.2 Company, rejoined from Divisional Rest Station.	
	5/10/18.		Feeding Strength :- 14,214.	
	6/10/18.		Feeding Strength :- 15,054. Nos. 1 and 2 Companies draw supplies from Railhead by M.T. and Nos. 3 and 4 Companies by H.T. T4/056912 Dr. Gillies, M., transferred from No.2 Company to No.4 Company. T4/422702 Dr. Masterbrook, W.J., from A.S.C. Base Dept and posted to No.2 Coy.	
	7/10/18.		Feeding Strength :- 15,162. T4/056981 Dr. Muddimer, A., transferred from No.1 Company to No.2 Company. T/309475 Dr. Eyre, W.C., transferred from No.1 Company to No.4 Company. T4/043706 Whr. Cpl. Buttler, admitted to 89th. Field Ambulance. Train Headquarters move from BRAKE CAMP to VLAMERTINGHE, Sheet 28/ H.2.d.8.0. Divisional Headquarters to Ramparts, YPRES.	
VLAMERTINGHE	8/10/18.		M.T. draw supplies from Railhead for all Companies.	
	9/10/18.		Feeding Strength :- 15, 086. T/11529 l/c. S.S.M. G.A. Fowle, No. 3 Company evacuated to No.2 C.C.S.	
	10/10/18.		Feeding Strength :- 15,886. 1. H.D. Animal from 18th. M.V.S. and taken on strength of No.4 Company.	
	11/10/18.		Feeding Strength :- 15,108. T4/28690 A/Sgt. Watts. G., No. 3 Company, appointed A/C.S.M. dated 23-9-1918, assumed duties 11-10-18, vice. T/13291 A/C.S.M. Grayburn, G., transferred to A.S.C. Malarial Units, ROUEN on 23-9-1918, authority A.S.C. P44/16967 dated 8-10-1918 and War Records CR/29805/A/18 dated 29-9-1918. T/28690 A/C.S.M. Watts, G., transferred to No.1 Company from No. 3 Company. Feeding Strength :- 15,494.	

Army Form C. 2118.

WAR DIARY
or
INTELLIGENCE SUMMARY.

(Erase heading not required.)

29th. Divisional Train.

Instructions regarding War Diaries and Intelligence Summaries are contained in F. S. Regs., Part II. and the Staff Manual respectively. Title pages will be prepared in manuscript.

Place	Date	Hour	Summary of Events and Information	Remarks and references to Appendices
	12/10/18.		Feeding Strength :@ 16,167.	
	13/10/18.		Feeding Strength :@ 15,939. T2nd. Lieut. W.E. Balmer, No.4 Company, granted leave to the U.K. from 13-10-18 to 27-10-18. Train Headquarters move to Ramparts, YPRES, 28/I.8.d.0.8.	
YPRES.	14/10/18.		Feeding Strength :- 15,783.	
	15/10/18.		Feeding Strength :- 15,191. Nos. 1,2,3, and 4 Companies move to Camps at 28/K.7.d.6.8., K.7.c.9.9., J.5.d.9.5. and J.12.a.4.8., respectively. Train Headquarters move from YPRES to 28/K.7.e.8.9.	
3/K.7.e.8.9.	16/10/18.		Feeding Strength :- 15,191. Train Headquarters move to LEDGEHEM - 28/L.8.A.5.9. Nos. 1.2.3 and 4 Companies move to 28/L&8&X&5&0., L.1.d.9.2., K.12.a.8.5., K.11.b.3.9. and L.7.d.1.9., respectively. Railhead changes from VLAMERTINGHE to ST.JEAN.	
LEDGEHEM.	17/10/18.		Feeding Strength :- 14,916. T4/035771 A/S.S.M. Pollard, E., No.2 Company, Temporary Promotion Duration of War, to T. S.S.M. effect from 2-5-1917, authority A.S.C. P43/16663/ dated 15th. Oct. 1918. S4/056862 A/Cpl. Kendall, W., No.4 Company, promoted Cpl. effect from 2-2-18, and T4/043832 A/L/Cpl. Speer, G., appointed L/Cpl. effect from 9-5-18, authority A.S.C. P43/16836 dated 15-10-18.	
	18/10/18.		Feeding Strength :- 14,906. T/30341 A/Cpl. Simmonds, R.J., No.2 Company, service with the colours extended to 7 years, authority A.S.C. 27237 dated 17-10-1918.	
	19/10/18.		Feeding Strength :- 14,749. Railhead to PASSCHENDAELE.	
	20/10/18.		Feeding Strength :- 14, 224. Train Headquarters move to 29/G.16.b8.2. Nos. 1,2,3, and 4 Coys. move to 29/G.16.d.7.3., G.16.d.7.3., G.23.a.1.9. and G.23.a.1.9. respectively. T4/11971 Sgt. McVicer, W.A., No.4 Company, admitted to 89th. Field Ambulance.	
GULLEGHEM.	21/10/1918		Feeding Strength :- 14,055. Train Headquarters move to COURTRAI. T4/85387 Dr. Blayney, D., No.1 Company, wounded by Shell Fire, died in 105th. Field Ambulance.	
COURTRAI.	22/10/18.		Feeding Strength :- 13,765. Nos. 1,2 and 3 Companies move to Camps at 29/H.15.b.5.2., H.20.a.5.4. and H.15.b.5.3. respectively. T2nd. Lieut. F.W. Martin, attached Central Purchase Board granted leave to U.K. from 22-10-18 5-11-18. T2nd. Lieut. J.S. Braegirdle, No.2 Coy., granted leave to the U.K. from 22-10-18 to 5-11-18. T.2nd. Lieut. A.B. Wells, No. 2 Coy., granted leave to U.K. from 22-10-18 to 5-11-18.	
	23/10/18.		Feeding Strength :- 13,357.	
	24/10/18.		Feeding Strength :- 13,687. T4/124120 Dr. Graham, D., and T4/043472 Dr. Ferguson, D., No.3 Coy., admitted to 87th. Field Ambulance. Railhead changes to BEYTHEM.	
	25/10/18.		Feeding Strength :- 13,708. Division being relieved by 31st. Division. No.2 Company move to New Area, staging the night 25th/26th. at RONCQ. T3/030706 L/Cpl. Tod, J. T4/043472 Dr.	

Army Form C. 2118.

WAR DIARY
or
~~INTELLIGENCE~~ SUMMARY.

29th. Divisional Train.

(Erase heading not required.)

Instructions regarding War Diaries and Intelligence Summaries are contained in F. S. Regs., Part II. and the Staff Manual respectively. Title pages will be prepared in manuscript.

Place	Date	Hour	Summary of Events and Information	Remarks and references to Appendices
	25/10/18.		Ferguson, D., and T4/124120 Dr. Graham, D., No. 3 Company, evacuated to C.C.S.	
	26/10/18.		Feeding Strength :- 13,333. No. 2 Company move from RONCQ to BONDUES. T/21747 A/Cpl. Grimshaw, H., T4/145783 Dr. Tomkins, B., T4/042862 Dr. Patrick, A., and SS/1653 Sgt. Whitbourne, G.W., No. 3 Company, evacuated to 36th. C.C.S. 86th. Infty. Bde. Group draw Supplies from ARMENTIERES.	
	27/10/18.		Feeding Strength, 11,226. T.2nd. Lieut. W.J.C. Thorold, No. 3 Company, granted leave to the U.K. from 27-10-18 to 10-11-18. Nos. 1,3. and 4 Companies move to new Area and Camp at 28/W.17.d, 7.9., 36/K.14.b.3.8. and 36/L.9.a.5.8. respectively. Train Headquarters move to 36/E.20.b.9.5. T4/119971 Sgt. McVicar, W.A. admitted to 89th. Field Ambulance 20-10-18, now struck off the strength. Railhead changes to ARMENTIERES.	
MOUVEAUX	28/10/18.		Feeding Strength :- 11,352.	
	29/10/18.		Feeding Strength :- 13,983.	
	30/10/18.		Feeding Strength :- 13,675.	
	31/10/1918.		Feeding Strength :- 13,282. S4/056723 Cpl. Bryant, A., and S4/056850 Cpl. Gomm, F., No.3 Company, admitted to 87th. Field Ambulance.	

[signature]

Lieut. Colonel, A.S.C.,
Commg., 29th. Divisional Train.

Army Form C. 2118.

WAR DIARY
or
INTELLIGENCE SUMMARY.
29th. DIVISIONAL TRAIN.

(Erase heading not required.)

Instructions regarding War Diaries and Intelligence Summaries are contained in F.S. Regs. Part II. and the Staff Manual respectively. Title pages will be prepared in manuscript.

Place	Date	Hour	Summary of Events and Information	Remarks and references to Appendices
MOUVEAUX.	1/11/18.		Railhead changes to MADALEINE. T4/044082 Cpl. W. Jardine, No.3 Coy. appointed A/Sgt. dated 11-6-18, with pay from 1-11-18 vice T4/037781 Sgt. Rogulski, A., transferred to R.A.F. dated 11-6-18. Authy: A.S.C. from No.1 Coy. P47/17675 dated 22-10-18. S4/090284 S.Sgt. Baldwin,H.E. evacuated to 36th. C.C.S. from No.1 Coy., dated 26-10-18. Feeding strength :- 15,515.	
	2/11/18.		Nos. 2 and 3 Coys. draw supplies from Railhead by H.T. Capt. A.S. Lee, No. 3 Coy. evacuated to No.II C.C.S., sick. T4/306545 Dr. Falkner, R., and T/422702 Dr. Easterbrook, W.J., No.2 Company admitted to 89th. Field Ambulance. T4/056981 Dr. Muddimer, A., No. 2 Company, to 36th. C.C.S. on 26-10-18. T/28573 Dr. Clark, H., and S4/056850 Cpl. Gomm, F., No. 3 Coy. evacuated to 11th. C.C.S. SS/1653 Sgt. Whitbourne, G.W. T3/030706 L/Cpl. Tod, J. and T4/145783 Dr. Tomkins, B., No. 3 Coy. rejoined Unit from 36th. C.C.S. 4 H.D. Animals drawn from 18th. M.V.S. Feeding Strength :- 14,320.	
	3/11/18.		Divisional Artillery move and No.1 Company move camp to s6/F.9.b.28. T4/422702 Dr. Easterbrook, W.J., No. 2 Coy. evacuated to 11th. C.C.S. Feeding Strength :- 15,575.	
	4/11/18. 5/11/18. 6/11/18.		T2/28573 Dr. Clark, H., evacuated to 11th. C.C.S. from No. 2 Coy. Feeding Strength :- 15,069. 1 Rider and 1 L.D. drawn from 18th. M.V.S. by No. 3 Coy. Feeding Strength :- 14,969. Division leaving XV Corps Area for X Corps Area. No. 4 Coy move to new area and camp at 29/T.12.c.1.9. T4/360545 Dr. Falkner, R., No. 2 Company rejoined Unit from Hospital. 1 H.D. animal evacuated from No. 3 Company to 18th. M.V.S. T4/042590 Dr. Hamlyn, W.J. to Military V.A.D. Hospital, ABBOTT, whilst on leave. Feeding Strength :- 13,792.	
ROLLEGHEM.	7/11/18.		Division move to New Area. Train Headquarters move to ROLLENGHEM – 29/T.2.a.2.5. No. 1 Company move to camp at 29/T.7.a.5.9. No. 3 Coy. move to 36/F.9.b.2.8. Supplies for Nos. 1, 3 and 4 Groups drawn by M.T. from Railhead. No 2 Group draw from Railhead by H.T. Feeding Strength :- 13, 611.	
	8/11/18.		No. 3 Coy. move to Camp at 29/T.6.d.7.0. No. 2 Coy. move to Camp at 29/S.29.a.4.5. All Supplies drawn frxxxxxx from Railhead by M.T. Feeding Strength :- 14,236.	
	10/11/18.		Train Headquarters move to 29/U.25.c.1.9. Nos. 1,2, 3 and 4 Companies move to 29/U.25.c.1.8. 29/T.11.b.6.1. CELLES, and 29/U.12.d.7.7. respectively. T4/111971 Sgt. McVicker, W.A. rejoined from A.S.C. Base Depot and posted to No.4 Coy. Feeding Strength 13,826.	
	11/11/18.		Nos. 3 and 4 Coys. move to Camps at 37/D.9.c.4.2. and 27/E.16.c.19. respectively. 7th. Aux. H.T. Company report to Division to assist in Transport work. Feeding Strength :- 13,823.	
	12/11/18.		Supplies for 88th. Infty. Bde. taken by 7th. Aux. H.T. Coy. to ANSERDEIL, refilling there, and taken on by Supply Wagons to ELLEZELLES; 1st. Line Transport and Baggage Wagons taking them from there to Unit. Supplies for 87th. Bde. taken by 7th. Aux: H.T. Coy., to No. 3 Coy's lines	

A7092   Wt. W128.9/M1293 750,000. 1/17. D.D. & L. Ltd. Forms/C.2118/14.

Army Form C. 2118.

WAR DIARY
or
INTELLIGENCE SUMMARY.

29th DIVISIONAL TRAIN.

(Erase heading not required.)

Instructions regarding War Diaries and Intelligence Summaries are contained in F.S. Regs., Part II. and the Staff Manual respectively. Title pages will be prepared in manuscript.

Place	Date	Hour	Summary of Events and Information	Remarks and references to Appendices
	12/11/18.		refilled, and taken to 1st. Line Transport by Supply Wagons. Nos. 1 and 2 Coys. refill in the ordinary way. Feeding Strength :- 14,888.	
RENAIX.	13/11/18.		Feeding Strength :- 16,037.	
	14/11/18.		Feeding Strength :- 14,433. Train Headquarters move to RENAIX.	
FLOBECQ.	15/11/18.		Train Headquarters move to FLOBECQ. Feeding Strength :- 16,201.	
	16/11/18.		Feeding Strength :- 15,726.	
	17/11/18.		S4/055658 S. Sgt. Taylor, S.W. No. 4 Coy., admitted to 88th. Field Ambulance. T/28573 Dr. Clark, H., rejoined No. 2 Company from Hospital. Feeding Strength :- 14,888.	
ENGHIEN.	18/11/18.		Feeding Strength :- 14,324. Train Headquarters move to ENGHIEN. Nos. 1, 2, 3 and 4 Coys. move to LE CAVE, CHISLENGHIEN, LOGE and HOVES respectively. S4/055658 S. Sgt. Taylor, S.W. evacuated to 64th. C.C.S.	
	19/11/18.		Feeding Strength :- 14,042.	
	20/11/18.		Feeding Strength :- 14,042.	
TUBIZE.	21/11/18.		Train Headquarters move to TUBIZE. Nos. 1, 2, 3 and 4 Coys. move to STEENKUP, GENETT, GENETTE, and CLABECQ respectively. Feeding Strength :- 13,807.	
	22/11/18.		Feeding Strength :- 14,026.	
	23/11/18.		T4/146748 L/Cpl. Brown, A., No.1 Coy., admitted to 2nd. Scottish General Hospital, whilst on leave to U.K. Feeding Strength :- 13,860.	
	24/11/18.		Feeding Strength :- 13,864.	
	25/11/18.		Feeding Strength :- 13,864.	
	26/11/18.		T4/240726 Dr. Vickery, H.P., No. 4 Coy., admitted 88th. Field Ambulance and evacuated to 17th. C.C.S. The following having arrive from the Base are posted to Companies :- T/437120 Dr. C'Garr, E., T4/18853 Dr. Newport, J.; T4/438942 Dr. Newton, H.C. to No. 3 Coy., and T/440619 Dr. Nicholl, A., to No. 2 Coy. T4/24987 Dr. Dillon, F.C., No.1 Company admitted 88th. Field Ambulance. Feeding Strength :- 13,883.	
	27/11/18.		T4/124987 Dr. Dillon, F.C. No.1 Company, evacuated to 26th. C.C.S. Feeding Strength :- 13,793.	
	28/11/18.		Feeding Strength :- 13,777.	
	29/11/18.		T4/088314 Dr. Copping, No.1 Coy., admitted to Canterbury Military Hospital whilst on leave to U.K. Feeding Strength :- 13,738.	
	30/11/18.		Feeding Strength :- 14,277.	

Lieut. Colonel, R.A.S.C.,
Comdg., 29th. Divisional Train.

Army Form C. 2118.

WAR DIARY
or
INTELLIGENCE SUMMARY.

29th Divisional Train.

(Erase heading not required.)

Dec Vol 34

Place	Date	Hour	Summary of Events and Information	Remarks and references to Appendices
	1/12/18.		S4/090284 S.Sgt. Baldwin, H.E. rejoined from Base and posted to No.1 Company. Feeding Strength :- 14,566.	
	2/12/18.		T. Capt. W.E.C. Hulme, R. 2nd. Lieut. A. Forbes and TS/9392 Dr. Sadd.Macroty, A., No. 4 Company, admitted to 88th. Field Ambulance. Feeding Strength :- 13,560.	
	3/12/18.		T.Capt. A.S. Lee., to U.K. sick, and struck off the strength dated 12-11-18. authority II Army QP/ASQ/21805/7. T. Capt. W.E.C. Hulme and TS/9392 Dr. Sadd. MacRory, A., No. 4 Company, evacuated to 44th. C.C.S. Feeding Strength :- 13,587.	
	4/12/18.		Feeding Strength :- 13,119.	
	5/12/18.		Feeding Strength :- 13,046.	
	6/12/18.		Feeding Strength :- 13,443.	
	7/12/18.		Feeding Strength :- 13,334.	
	8/12/18.		T4/24072 6 Dr. Vickery, No. 4 Coy., rejoined from Hospital. Feeding Strength :- 13,104.	
	9/12/18.		Feeding Strength :- 13,052.	
	10/12/18.		T/30341 A/Cpl. Simmonds, R., promoted Cpl. to date from 21-6-15 to complete original establishment - authy: ASQ/P45/17312/403. Feeding Strength :- 13,810.	
	11/12/18.		T/28080 A/C.S.M. Waits, G., promoted C.S.M. with effect from 23-9-18 and T/27455 A.Cpl. Squires, T.F., to Cpl. with effect from 9-11-18 Authy: A.S.C./P45/16312/403 dated 26-11-18. Feeding Strength :- 13,225.	
	12/12/18.		Feeding strength :- 12,439.	
	13/12/18.		T. 2nd. Lieut. A. Forbes, Rejoined No. 4 Company from Hospital. T/20683 A/C.S.M. Bland, J.T., No. 4 Coy., promoted C.S.M. with effect from 5-9-17 - athy: ASC/P45/17312/403 dated 26-11-18. Feeding Strength :- 12,717.	
	14/12/18.		Feeding strength :- 12,662.	
	15/12/18.		Feeding strength :- 14,103.	
	16/12/18.		T4/162037 Cpl. Wilson, R., No. 3 Coy., T/438542 Dr. Nurse, J., T/423729 Dr. Ogilvie, T., from A.S.G. Base Depot. Feeding Strength :- 12,534.	
	17/12/18.		Feeding Strength :- 12,778.	
	18/12/18.		T/18919 A/C.S.M. Stevens, F., promoted T/C.S.M. 29-1-18, athy:- RASC/P45/17312/403 dated 29-1-18. Feeding Strength :- 14503.	
	19/12/18.		Feeding Strength :- 12,860.	
	20/12/18.		T4/088799 Dr. Bellman, J.H. from 88th. Infty. Bde. H.Q. to No. 4 Coy., T/364914 Dr. Dalton, W., from No. 4 Coy., to 88th. Infty. Bde. H.Q. Feeding Strength :- 12,818.	
	21/12/18.		Lieut. Colonel. E.T.L. Wright, D.S.O. Commanding Train, granted 30 days special leave to U.K. athy:- 2nd. Corps A.C./2327/ dated 24-11-18. Feeding Strength :- 14,531.	

Army Form C. 2118.

WAR DIARY
or
INTELLIGENCE SUMMARY. 29th. Divisional Train.

(Erase heading not required.)

Instructions regarding War Diaries and Intelligence Summaries are contained in F. S. Regs., Part II. and the Staff Manual respectively. Title pages will be prepared in manuscript.

Place	Date	Hour	Summary of Events and Information	Remarks and references to Appendices
	22/12/18.		Feeding Strength :- 13,832.	
	23/12/18.		T4/042590 Dr. Hamlyn, W.J., admitted to Hospital in U.K. whilst on leave dated 5-11-18. Feeding Strength :- 14,391.	
	24/12/18.		T/440619 Dr. Nicholl, A.C. and T/231512 Dr. Haigh, W.H. to 89th. Field Ambulance. Feeding Strength :- 14,402.	
	25/12/18.		The following reinforcements arrived from A.S.C. Base Depot and posted to Companies :- T5/8199 Farr, S.Sgt. Shaw, H., Pte. Gibbons, G.S., T4/086338 Dr. Robertson, D., T4/276980 Dr. Posher, W.E., T4/059636 Dr. Plows, H., T5/SR/02159 Dr. Irons, T.R. to No. 3 Coy., T/261512 Dr. Haigh, W.H., T/386485 Dr. Horner, G., T/406149 Dr. Holdam, P., T/343212 Dr. Henderson, J., T/260883 Dr. Hirst, G.T., to No. 2 Coy., T4/088701 Dr. Hann, P., T4/058658 Dr. Harding, W.E., T4/233006 Dr. Honeybul, G., to No. 1 Coy. Feeding Strength :- 15,008.	
	26/12/18.		T/364914 Dr. Dalton, W., transferred from 88th. Infty. Bde. H.Q. to No. 4 Coy., and T/38895 Dr. Cushion, S., to 88th. Infty Bde., H.Q., from No.4 Coy. Feeding Strength :- 15,676.	
	27/12/18.		T4/093231 Dr. Lock, F.A., admitted 3rd. Southern General Hospital, Oxford, whilst on leave. Feeding Strength :- 15,162.	
	28/12/18.		The following proceeded to U.K. for demobilization :- T3/025725 Sadd. Cpl. Hunter, R., T4/044528 D. Anderton, W.T., No.2 Coy., T5/620 Dr. Martin, W., No. 4 Coy. Feeding Strength :- 14,900. The following proceeded to U.K. for demobilization T4/056912 Dr. Gilles, M.F., T2/12577 Dr. Jones, T.J., T4/042637 Dr. Jenkins, S., T4/061993 dr. Parker, J.F., No. 4 Company. Feeding Strength :- 14,580.	
	30/12/18.		T/21283 Dr. Streamer, F.C. admitted to Hospital from No. 4 Coy. The following proceeded to U.K. for demobilization :- T4/042082 A/Sgt. Jardine, W., T2/14833 Dr. Graham, A., No. 3 Coy., T3/02 3759 Dr. Goates, R., No. 2 Coy. Feeding Strength :- 14,301.	
	31/12/18.		The following arrived from R.A.S.C. Base Depot and posted to Coys :- T3/028771 Dr. Swan, L., T4/213099 Dr.Smith, J.W., to No. 4 Coy. T/33308 Dr. Brazier, J.P., transferred to 88th. Infty. Bde. H.Q., from No. 4 Coy. Feeding Strength :- 15,302.	

Lieut. Colonel, R.A.S.C.,
Commg., Southern Divisional Train.

**RHINE ARMY
SOUTHERN DIVISION
LATE 29TH DIVISION**

DIVISIONAL TRAIN R.A.S.C.
JAN - OCT 1919

2070 & 2084

Army Form C. 2118.

WAR DIARY
or
INTELLIGENCE SUMMARY.
(Erase heading not required.)

Instructions regarding War Diaries and Intelligence Summaries are contained in F. S. Regs., Part II. and the Staff Manual respectively. Title pages will be prepared in manuscript.

29th. Divisional Train.

Place	Date	Hour	Summary of Events and Information	Remarks and references to Appendices
ODENTHAL, GERMANY.	1/1/19.		Feeding Strength :- 14,253. The following reinforcements arrived from Base Depot :- T1/1514 Dr. Scott, C.M., T3/027084 Dr. Shimmin, J., T3/028548 Dr. Snaden, J., T4/211594 Dr. Smith, J.W., T4/260036 Dr. Steer, F.G., T4/259452 Dr. Steer, R.N., T4/037917 Dr. Stevens, H.C., T1/1546 Dr. Strudwick, F.A.	
	2/1/19.		Feeding Strength :- 13,948. T3/4347 Farr. S.Sgt. Jones, A.I. struck off the strength of B.E.F. as from 27-10-18 - athy: RASC. L14/10223 dated 31-21-18.	
	3/1/19.		Feeding Strength :- 14,257. T. Capt. W.E.C. Hulme to U.K. and struck off the strength dated 15-12-18 - athy: 20/G.H.	
	4/1/19.		Feeding Strength :- 14,487. S4/060489 Cpl. H.C. Ludgate, No.1 Coy., evacuated to 44th. C.C.S. T.2nd. Lieut. A.A. Beer, No.1 Coy., struck off the strength - athy: RASC/22145 dated 13-1-19.	
	5/1/19.		Feeding Strength :- 13,819. T4/127375 Cpl. Roffe, R., from Base Depot and posted to No. 3 Cov.	
	6/1/19.		Feeding Strength :- 13,705. T/212283 Dr. Streamer, F.C. admitted to Hospital. T/343212 Lr. Henderson, T., T/260868 Dr. Hurst, G.F., and T3/028548 Dr. Snaden,J., No.2 Coy., transferred to No.1 Coy. S4/216154 Pte. Philpot, T.W., demobilized whilst on leave to U.K. - athw: RASC/M/39/408 dated 15-1-19.	
	7/1/19.		Feeding Strength :- 13,656. Lieut. W.J.C. Thorold, No. 3 Coy., granted 14 days leave to U.K. and demobilized.	
	8/1/19.		Feeding Strength :- 13,838. T5/7540 Whr.Cpl. Gillham, G., evacuated to 64th. C.C.S. S4/090284 Sgt. Baldwin, H.E., No.1 Coy., demobilized whilst on leave	
	9/1/19.	S	Feeding Strength :- 14,210. T. 2nd. Lieut. J.H. Hollowell evacuated to U.K. dated 21-12-18.- athy: 72/GH.List No. 1360 dated 2-1-18. T/437120 Dr. O'Garr, No. 3 Coy., transferred to 88th. Field Ambulance.	
	10/1/19.		Feeding Strength :- 14,268. S4/159150 Sgt. J.L. Frith, No. 4 Coy., mentioned in Despatches, New Year Honour Lists of 1919. S4/056850 Cpl. Gonum, F., from Base Depot and posted to No.3 Coy. T4/160929 Dr. Rose, T.W. Demobilized whilst on leave.	
	11/1/19.		Feeding Strength :- 13,817. S4/060489 Cpl. H.C. Ludlage, No.1 Coy., from 44th. C.C.S.	
	12/1/19.		Feeding Strength :- 13,763. T. S.S.M. T. Mole, No. 4 Coy., awarded the Belgian Croix de Guerre. athy. 2nd. Army Wire No. FD/39 dated 7-1-19. T4/146708 L/Cpl. Brown, A., demobilized whilst on leave.	
	13/1/19.		Feeding Strength :- 13,786. T5/8362 Farr. S. Sgt. Hurren, A., and T/260883 Dr. Hursty G.T. evacuated to 36th. C.C.S.	
	14/1/19.		Feeding Strength:- 13,488. Major K.R.C. Holman, No. 1 Coy., demobilized whilst on leave dated 31-12-18.	
	15/1/19.		Feeding Strength :- 13,553. T1/1488 Dr. Sadd. Jeffrey, T., from Base Depot and posted to 4 Coy.	

Army Form C. 2118.

WAR DIARY
or
INTELLIGENCE SUMMARY.
(Erase heading not required.)

29th. Divisional Train.

Instructions regarding War Diaries and Intelligence Summaries are contained in F. S. Regs., Part II. and the Staff Manual respectively. Title pages will be prepared in manuscript.

Place	Date	Hour	Summary of Events and Information	Remarks and references to Appendices
	15/1/19.		T3/8631 Sadd. Cpl. Briggs, H., No.1 Coy., admitted 88th. Field Ambulance. T2/14802 Farr. Cpl. Bennett, G.H. demobilized whilst on leave. T/370698 Dr. Curzon, J., demobilized whilst on leave.	
	16/1/19.		Feeding Strength :- 15,333. T. 2nd. Lieut. A.R. Wells, No. 2 Coy., granted leave to U.K. for 14 days.	
	17/1/19.		Feeding Strength :- 13,345. T4/059654 Dr. Jones, A., to U.K. for demobilization. T4/263737 Dr. Jordan, G., evacuated to 62nd. C.C.S. S4/159150 Sgt. Frith, J.L. No. 4 Coy., demobilized whilst on leave.- Athy. RASC/M39/559 dated 4-2-19.	
	18/1/19.		Feeding Strength :- 13279. T4/159832 Dr. Sadd. Phillips, F.H. from Base Depot and posted to No. 2 Coy. T5/030854 Dpr. Angus, A., evacuated to 64th. C.C.S. from No. 3 Coy.	
	19/1/19.		Feeding Strength :- 13216.	
	20/1/19.		Feeding Strength :- 13014. T4/042573 Dr. Drake, F., and T4/161531 Dr. Rumble, J., to U.K. for Demobilization and struck off the strength.	
	21/1/19.		Feeding Strength :- 13182. T. 2nd. Lieut. P.D. Cornwell, from RASC Base Depot and posted to No.1 Coy. athy. Army ST(P) 1551/860.	
	22/1/19.		Feeding Strength :- 12743. S4/055656 S.Sgt. Taylor rejoined from Hospital to No.1 Coy. T3/8631 Sadd. Briggs, H., evacuated to 36th. C.C.S. from No.1 Coy. T.2nd. Lieut. J.A. James, from RASC Base Depot and posted to No. 3 Coy.- athy. 2nd. Army ST(P) 1551/873 dated 21-1-19.	
	23/1/19.		Feeding Strength :- 12200.	
	24/1/19.		Feeding Strength :- 12137.	
	25/1/19.		Feeding Strength :- 12284.	
	26/1/19.		Feeding Strength :- 12116.	
	27/1/19.		Feeding Strength :- 11920. T4/057369 Dr. Murdoch, A., to U.K. for demobilization.	
	28/1/19.		Feeding Strength :- 11889.	
	29/1/19.		Feeding Strength :- 11695.	
	30/1/19.		Feeding Strength :- 11531.	
	31/1/19.		Feeding Strength :- 11573. T.Capt. W.H. King granted 30 days leave to U.K. Capt. C.E. Browne, M.O. granted 30 days leave to U.K.	

Lieut. Colonel, R.A.S.C.,
Comdg., 29th. Divisional Train.

Army Form C. 2118.

WAR DIARY
or
INTELLIGENCE SUMMARY.
(Erase heading not required.)

SOUTHERN DIVISIONAL TRAIN.

Instructions regarding War Diaries and Intelligence Summaries are contained in F.S. Regs., Part II. and the Staff Manual respectively. Title pages will be prepared in manuscript.

Place	Date	Hour	Summary of Events and Information	Remarks and references to Appendices
ODENTHAL, GERMANY.	1/2/19.		Feeding Strength :- 11,579.	
	2/2/19.		Feeding Strength :- 11,466. T4/160927 Dr. Rose, T.W., demobilized whilst on leave dated 10-1-19.	
	3/2/19.		Feeding Strength :- 11,463. T4/146748 1/Cpl. Brown, A., demobilized whilst on leave dated 12-1-19. T3/026742 Cpl. Luff, F.C. No.1 Coy., evacuated 64th. C.C.S. T.Capt. R.C.O. Viveash transferred to 1 Coy from No.2 Coy. Capt. R.W.A. Hedger Transferred from No.1 Coy. to No.2 Coy.	
	4/2/19.		Feeding Strength :- 11380.	
	5/2/19.		Feeding Strength :- 11380. M2/147648 Pte. Hill, B., evacuated to 44th. C.C.S. dated 21-1-19.	
	6/2/19.		Feeding Strength :- 11071. T4/212061 SSM. Liming, F.M., from 74th. Divisional Train and posted to No. 3 Coy.	
	7/2/19.		Feeding Strength :- 11132. T1/2732 Sgt. Cooper, T.W., and T2/14168 Cpl. Gillard, L.E., from 87th. Field Ambulance to No. 3 Coy.	
	8/2/19.		Feeding Strength :- 10985.	
	9/2/19.		Feeding Strength :- 11274.	
	10/2/19.		Feeding Strength :- 10748.	
	11/2/19.		The following proceeded to U.K. for demobilization :- T4/244401 Dr. Wiggins,A., No.4 Coy., T4/042234 Dr. Far. Walter, R.R., T4/036936 Dr.Davidson,S., and T4/057009 Dr. Findlay, C., No.3 Coy., T4/042455 Cpl. Jennings, T., No. 2 Coy., T/32225 Dr. Browning, A., from 87th. Field Ambulance to No.2 Coy. Major C.G. Taylor granted 14 days special leave to U.K.	
	12/2/19.		Feeding Strength :- 10887. The following proceeded to U.K. for demobilization :- T4/160957 CQMS Stanley, P.C., T4/043297 Dr. Arden, T.E., T4/043297 Dr. Bagshaw, W., T4/145751 Dr. Velvic, C., No.1 Company.	
	13/2/19.		Feeding Strength :- 11712. T4/158762 Dr. Pearson, G.E., No.1 Coy., evacuated to 44th. C.C.S.	
	14/2/19.		Feeding Strength :- 106664. T/392000 Dr. Ritchie, T.T. No. 4 Coy., evacuated to 36th. C.C.S. T4/160959 Dr. Middleton,No.1 Coy., to 36th. C.C.S.	
	15/2/19.		Feeding Strength :- 10398. S4/056879 A/S.Sgt. Sandiford, F., transferred from No.3 Coy to XX. No.1 Coy.	
	16/2/19.		Feeding Strength :- 10,527. T3/028890 Dr. Clements, A., from No. 4 Coy., to 88th. Infty. Bde., H.Q. T3/33308 Dr. Brazier, J., from 88th. Infty. Bde. H.Q., to No. 4 Coy.	
	17/2/19.		Feeding Strength :- 10014.	
	18/2/19.		Feeding Strength :- 10885.	
	19/2/19.		Feeding Strength :- 12095.	
	20/2/19.		Feeding Strength :- 11032. T/18525 T.SSM. Mole, T., and T/17116 Sadd. S. Sgt. Mortimer, F., to U.K. for dispersal from No. 4 Coy. T25032 Dr. Cuthbert, J., T4/042700 Dr. Sayers, D.M. No.3	

Army Form C. 2118.

WAR DIARY
or
INTELLIGENCE SUMMARY
(Erase heading not required.)

SOUTHERN DIVISIONAL TRAIN.

Instructions regarding War Diaries and Intelligence Summaries are contained in F. S. Regs., Part II. and the Staff Manual respectively. Title pages will be prepared in manuscript.

Place	Date	Hour	Summary of Events and Information	Remarks and references to Appendices
	20/2/19.		Coy., T4/044068 Cpl. Freestone, H.C., No.1 Coy., to U.K. for demobilization.	
	21/2/19.		T. Capt. R.C.O. Viveash, granted 14 days special leave to U.K. T/206683 T.C.S.M. Bland, J.T., No.4 Coy., transferred to 1st. Divisional Train. Feeding Strength :- 11,205.	
	22/2/19.		Feeding Strength :- 11,206.	
	23/2/19.		Feeding Strength :- 11,032.	
	24/2/19.		Feeding Strength :- 11,534.	
	25/2/19.		Feeding Strength :- 11,429. The following proceeded to U.K. for demobilization :- S4/056865 Cpl. Kendall, W., S/385679 Pte. Gibbons, G.S., No.4 Coy., and T4/127375 Cpl. Roffe, R., No. 3 Coy.	
	26/2/19.		Feeding Strength :- 11,397. The following proceeded to U.K. for demobilization :- CHT/1108 Wgr. Birmington, V., T4/144226 Dr. Beevor, N., No.1 Coy., T1/22501 Dr. Simper, G., No. 2 Coy.	
	27/2/19.		Feeding Strength :- 11,540.	
	28/2/19.		Feeding Strength :- 11,548. T. Capt. W. Campbell from 14th. Divisional Train and posted to No.1 Company.	

Lieut. Colonel, R.A.S.C.,
Commg., Southern Divisional Train.

Confidential

War Diary of

Southern (late 29th) Divisional Train

from 1/3/19 to 31/3/19

Volume 1

Londilon Divisional Train
(Late 29th Div Train)

March 1919

VOL. 1. p. 1.

Army Form C. 2118.

WAR DIARY
or
INTELLIGENCE SUMMARY.
(Erase heading not required.)

Instructions regarding War Diaries and Intelligence Summaries are contained in F. S. Regs., Part II. and the Staff Manual respectively. Title pages will be prepared in manuscript.

Place	Date	Hour	Summary of Events and Information	Remarks and references to Appendices
Cologne	1/3/19		Capt R.C.O VIVEASH transf from no 1 to No 3 Co.	
			Capt C.E. BROWNE. M.C. Adjt struck off the strength after over 30 days absence on leave to United Kingdom	
	3/3/19		1. O.R. demobilized whilst on leave to U.K. and struck off strength	
	4/3/19		1 OR died from gun shot wound, self inflicted. 1 OR to hospital	
	6/3/19		2 OR to Concentration Camps for demobilisation	
	8/3/19		7 OR do	
	9/3/19		1 OR demobilised whilst on leave to U.K. and struck off strength	
	10/3/19		2 OR to hospital	
	11/3/19		T/2nd Lieut J.A JAMES granted 14 days leave to U.K.	
			T/Lieut J.W. MARTIN to UK for demobilisation	
	12/3/19		1 OR demobilised whilst on leave to U.K and struck off strength	
	13/3/19		1 OR do	
	14/3/19		1 O.R. discharged from hospital	
	15/3/19		4 OR to Concentration Camps for demobilisation	

O.V.

Southern Divisional Train
(late 29th Divl Train)

VOL. I. p. 2

Army Form C. 2118.

WAR DIARY
or
INTELLIGENCE SUMMARY.
(Erase heading not required.)

Instructions regarding War Diaries and Intelligence Summaries are contained in F.S. Regs., Part II. and the Staff Manual respectively. Title pages will be prepared in manuscript.

Place	Date	Hour	Summary of Events and Information	Remarks and references to Appendices
Oamhut	16/3/19		2 O.R. to hospital. 1 O.R. joined from Base	
	17/3/19		1 O.R. demobilised whilst on leave and struck off strength	
	18/3/19		Lieut E.W. BALMER granted 14 days leave to U.K.	
	20/3/19		1 O.R. died, gunshot wound (self inflicted)	
	21/3/19		T/Major C.T.C. BEECROFT. D.S.O. from 14th Div. Train joined for duty as S.S.O. 1 O.R. joined from Div Signal Co. 1 O.R. to hospital. 1 O.R. to Concentration Camp for demobilisation	
	22/3/19		1 O.R. from 58 Div. Train. 1 O.R. from 14th Div Train	
	25/3/19		T/Capt. W.P.C. FRANKS to 14th Div Train. 1 O.R. from 58th Div Train. 1 O.R. from hospital	
	26/3/19		1 O.R. to hospital	
	27/3/19		Major (T/Lt-Col) C. HULL D.S.O. from 8th Div Train in relief of Major (a/Lt-Col) E.T.L. WRIGHT. D.S.O.	
	28/3/19		Major (T/Lt-Col) C. HULL D.S.O. assumes command of Southern Div Train vice Major (a/Lt-col) E.T.L. WRIGHT to England. 1 O.R. to Concentration camp for demobilisation	
	31/3/19		T/Lieut A.B. WELLS to 15th Div Train. 17 O.R. from Base	

Confidential

War Diary of

Southern (late 29th) Divisional Train.

From

1/4/19 to 30/4/19.

Volume II.

"Southern" Divisional Train
(late 29th Div. Train)

April 1919
Army Form C. 2118.

Vol I Page 3.

WAR DIARY
or
INTELLIGENCE SUMMARY.
(Erase heading not required.)

Instructions regarding War Diaries and Intelligence Summaries are contained in F.S. Regs., Part II. and the Staff Manual respectively. Title pages will be prepared in manuscript.

Place	Date	Hour	Summary of Events and Information	Remarks and references to Appendices
ODENTHAL	1/4/19		4 O.R. from 4th Divisional Train. 3 Horses and 2 mules from 8th Div. Train.	
			1 O.R. to C.C.S. 36 horses and 1 mule to Army Collecting Camp	
	2/4/19		7 O.R. from Base	
	3/4/19		T 2/28 J.S. Breezgirdle transferred from No 2 Coy to No 3 Coy	
			1 O.R. from 8th Divisional Train. 1 O.R. from Base.	
			1 O.R. to 4th C.C.S.	
	4/4/19		T 2/28 J.S. Breezgirdle No 3 Coy proceeded leave to U.K. for 14 days.	
			T 2/35 A Crouch from 15 Brit. Train.	
			1 O.R. to 6th Field Amb. from No 4 Coy.	
	6/4/19		1 O.R. evac. to 6th C.C.S. from No 4 Coy died.	
	7/4/19		1 O.R. from 4th Div. Train.	
	8/4/19		1 O.R. from 32nd Southern Inf. Bde. to No 4 Coy. 1 O.R. from No 4 Coy to 8th Infantry Bde.	
			1 Major W.H. Preston from 47th Div. Train.	
			1 Capt. L. Spanton from 14th Div. Train.	
			1 Capt. W.A. King to Concentration Camp for Demob.	
			1 O.R. to Concentration Camp for Demob.	
			3 O.R. to Hospital	
			1 O.R. to 3rd Infantry Bde.	
			1 Horse from 18 M.V.S.	

APRIL 1919
Army Form C. 2118.

Vol I Page 4
SOUTHERN DIV TRAIN
(INF 29th DIV TRAIN)

WAR DIARY
or
INTELLIGENCE SUMMARY.
(Erase heading not required.)

Place	Date	Hour	Summary of Events and Information	Remarks and references to Appendices
ADEN KHOR	9/4/19		1 OR from 57th Div Train posted to No 4 Coy.	
	10/4/19		13 Horses from 15th Middlesex R.	
	12/4/19		T/Capt W Campbell granted 14 days leave to U.K. I/Lt E.W. Barmen demobilised whilst on leave to U.K. Struck off Strength on/from 11/4/19. 1 OR to 37th C.C.S.	
	13/4/19		1 OR to 64th C.C.S.	
	14/4/19		T/Capt. J.O. Power from 2nd Div Train 1 OR from S. Divisional HQ. 1 Horse from 16 M.V.S.	
	15/4/19		17 ORs from Guard Div Train.	
	17/4/19		1 OR to 64 C.C.S. 2 ORs from 57 Div Train	
	19/4/19		6 ORs to Concentration Camp for Demob	
	21/4/19		T/Capt A.C. Best from 17th Div Train.	
	29/4/19		65 R Horses from 12th Squadron Remounts. 19 R to 99th M.G. Coy. 15 R to Divisional Signal Coy.	
	30/4/19		10 R to 154 S. Infantry Bde. 10 to II Infantry Bde. 10 to III Infantry Bde.	OH

April 1919

Vol I PAGE 5

Southern Divl Train
(1st 29th Divl Train)

WAR DIARY
or
INTELLIGENCE SUMMARY.
(Erase heading not required.)

Army Form C. 2118.

Instructions regarding War Diaries and Intelligence Summaries are contained in F. S. Regs., Part II. and the Staff Manual respectively. Title pages will be prepared in manuscript.

Place	Date	Hour	Summary of Events and Information	Remarks and references to Appendices
24/4/19 Devonport	24/4/19		2/Lt F.N Greer struck off lists to U.K. date 31/3/19	
			7/Capt R. Hedger do date 5/4/19	
	25/4/19		1 O.R. to Southern Div H.Q	
	26/4/19		13 H.D Horses received from So. Div. Artillery	
			5 L.D do	
	27/4/19		2 O.R. leave to U.K.	
	28/4/19		2 O.R. to 85th Field Amb	
	29/4/19			
	30/4/19			

p. 5

May 1919   Vol. I

WAR DIARY Southern Civil Train   Army Form C. 2118.

INTELLIGENCE SUMMARY.
(Erase heading not required.)

Place	Date 1919	Hour	Summary of Events and Information	Remarks and references to Appendices
Ostenthal	May 1		4 prisoners reported from 38th O.P.A. Bets. taken on strength of No.1 Coy. 32 H.D. taken on strength of No.1 Coy. from 38th O.P.A. Bde.	
	2		7 O.R. b/U.K. for Demobilization taken off strength of No.1 Coy. One O.R. from hospital and 2 O.R. admitted to Hospital 1 Coy. 3 O.R. b/U.K. for Demobilization taken off strength of 2 Coy. 1 O.R. b/U.K. Devoet from No.3 Coy. No.4 Coy. 1 O.R. admitted to Hospital. 6 O.R. b/U.K. for Demobilization 1 O.R. proceeded on leave.	
	3		No. 1 Coy. 2 O.R. from Hospital. No. 4 Coy. 1	
	4		No. 1 Coy. 2 recd. Courses M.R. a Leave 6 U.K. 1 O.R. from Hospital. No. 2 Coy. 2 H.D. Leave to 16 Mar U.S.	
	5		No. 1 Coy. 1 O.R. from Hospital. No. 2 Coy. 1 O.R. to 88 Field Amb. for duty.	
	6		No. 1 Coy. 1 officer 3 Coy. et - 2 Coy. 1 R. Horse 278 M.W. Specialization No.4 Coy. 1 O.R. to Hospital	
	7		No. 1 Coy. Lieut Colp + Capt C.E. Browne M.C. taken on strength as from 1/5/19	
	8		No. 1 Coy. 1 O.R. to Hospital. 3 Coy. reported one adm to 4 & 7 Field Amb.	
	9		No. 2 Coy. 1 O.R. demobilized sent to leave b/U.K. 27-1-19. No. 4 Coy. 2 O.R. by 3 rd Swallow ref. Ret. to duty	
	10		No. 1 Coy. 2 L.D. leave to 3 Coy. 2 Coy. 2 O.R. on leave b/U.K. 3 Coy. 2 L.D. leave from ret. to duty.	
	11		No. 1 Coy. 1 O.R. proceeded on leave ret. to duty. 1 other Coy. 1 O.R. leave b/U.K. 1 O.R. 3 Coy. 1 O.R. on leave b/U.K. 1 L.D. leave transferred to 1 Coy.	
			No. 8 Coy. No. 2 Field amb. Ret. to duty. 1 other Coy.	

WAR DIARY

May 1919. Vol 1 Northern Bul Tam p.6

Army Form C. 2118.

INTELLIGENCE SUMMARY

(Erase heading not required.)

Place	Date 1919	Hour	Summary of Events and Information	Remarks and references to Appendices
Odenthal	May 12		4th Coy 20 Bn leaves BWR. 8 OR K&Ren on strength from 113 Bde RFA. 8 OR K&Ren on strength from 126 hdz RFA. 30R to MR for demobilisation. 3 LD leaves 148 days HQ Bn Lovat to HQ on Concentration Camp strength of 1 Sgt & 8 OR. 48 D leaves from 113 Bde RFA. 74 D leaves from 126 hdz RFA taken on strength. No 3 Coy 2 OR BWR for demobilisation.	
	13		No 1 Coy 1 OR from hospital. 1 OR from 38 Div ATC taken on strength from 113 Bde RFA. No 2 Coy 1 OR BWR for demobilisation.	
	14		No 1 Coy Draft at Witzerad joined from 8 Div. Strain taken on strength 12/5/19. 1 OR from 113 Bde 1 OR from 126 hdz RFA. Return on strength 12/5/19. 10R on leave BWR. 2 Coy Capt CNT Jennings joined from 8 Bn. Train leaves on strength 12/5/19. Lt. 3 Coy. Capt J.R. Sharples on leave to UK. 1 OR transferred to 9 H R to Cologne. 2 R & D leaves to 24th MVS.	
	15		4th Coy 1 OR transferred to HR Cologne. 2 R & 22 HD leaves to 24th MVS. 2 Coy. 10 Bn leaves UK. 1 OR from 61st CCS 14/5/19.	
	16		4th Coy 1 OR admitted hospital. 1 OR attached from 9th Res Regt. 1 R leave from UK on return to No 3 Coy 2 OR to hospital. No 4 Coy 1 OR admitted to hospital.	
	17		No 1 Coy 6 OR attached from 5 Py Warwick Regt. 10 HD Lorries & Scotland Wig. 3 on attack of Plymouth through No 2 Coy 30 Bn leaves UK. 1 OR transferred from 2 Coy. 4th Coy 1 OR transferred from 2 Coy.	

WAR DIARY

May 1919 VOL I Southern Rwl Train P 7

Army Form C. 2118.

Instructions regarding War Diaries and Intelligence Summaries are contained in F. S. Regs., Part II. and the Staff Manual respectively. Title pages will be prepared in manuscript.

INTELLIGENCE SUMMARY
(Erase heading not required.)

Place	Date 1919	Hour	Summary of Events and Information	Remarks and references to Appendices
Odenthal	May 18		No 1 Coy 30 Bn leave b/UK. 20R b/UK for demobilization. No 2 Coy 10R from hospital. 10R b/UK for demobilization of No 3 Coy 40R b/UK for demobilization No 4 Coy 14D home transferred to 51st Hands Regt.	
	19		No 1 Coy 1R recd 2nd Smith Inf Bde 1pr Bn. of No 3 Coy 20R on leave b/UK. 1 L D Rewnch 24 MVS 1R home NRE	
			No 1 Coy 20R on leave b/UK	
	20		No 1 Coy 20R from Hospital. 10R b/UK on leave. No 2 Coy 20R on leave b/UK. No 3 Coy recd Sprgeant L.	
			Transferred from 89 Field Ambce b/UK 3 C&S 19/5/19. No 2 Coy 20R on leave b/UK. of No 4 Coy 20R on leave b/UK	
			No 1 Coy 10R transferred to hospital 1 HD Rewnch 148 MVS 11 HD Lane 187 Field Ambce of No 2 Coy 10R from	
	21		leave b/UK. 1 R attached to hospital 1 HD Rewnch. No 2 Coy 20R on leave b/UK. 10R transferred from 89 Field Ambce to 64 CCS.	
	22		No 1 Coy 1R on leave b/UK. 30R attacked from 57 Inf Regt. Rewnch & 9 Ok Pr 52 My 1 Warwick Regt.	
	23		No 1 Coy 24 D Rewnch 57 Warr Regt 14 D Rewnch 1st South Wales B.	
	24		No 1 Coy 20R on leave b/UK. 1 OR demob. Not to return leave to UK. Capt G P Dougherty proceed from	
			358 M T Coy 20/5/19. 1 L D Rewnch 87 Field Ambce 11 D 18 MVS No 4 Coy 10R discharged whilst	
			on leave b/UK 10/1/19	
	25		No 1 Coy 20R on leave b/UK. 2 Pr Rattached from 52 Warr Regt of No 2 Coy 4 OR b/UK for leave on	
			No 3 Coy 10R discharged from 64 CCS. No 4 Coy 10R to 3rd South Inf Bde for duty.	

Army Form C. 2118.

May 1919 - Vol I WAR DIARY Southern Rwl Train 1.8

INTELLIGENCE SUMMARY

(Erase heading not required.)

Instructions regarding War Diaries and Intelligence Summaries are contained in F. S. Regs., Part II. and the Staff Manual respectively. Title pages will be prepared in manuscript.

Place	Date 1919	Hour	Summary of Events and Information	Remarks and references to Appendices
Secunderabad	May 7		No 1 Coy. 14 OR MR for demobilization. 20 R on leave 6 WK. 10 R attached from 52 Cavalry Regt	
			admitted to Hospital. 10 R discharged from Hospital. No 1 Coy 9 0 R.h 6 WK Concert.	
	27		No 1 Coy 10 R on leave 6 WK. 11 O R attached from 9 Cav. Regt. 1 O R.returned to Hospital. 2 O R. 1 WK	
			demobilized. No 2 Coy 8·1·19. No 3 Coy Sergt I Beaumont returned duty from	
			No 3 CCS. 10 R from 81 Field Amb. 1 O R 1 WK for transfer to 20 R on leave 6 WK.	
	28		No 1 Coy Capt & Adjt. G E Browne M.C. who has been on leave 6 WK from received overseas...	
			absence of absent Capt 29·3·19. 6 OR attached from 9 Cav Regt. 1 O R from 51st Hants Regt 9 OR.	
			attached from 51st Hants Regt. No 4 Coy. 10 R on leave 6 WK	
	29		No 1 Coy. 20 R on leave 6 WK. No 4 Coy. 1 R admitted to 58th Field Amb.	
	30		No 1 Coy. Capt. J P Thompson k Reg.t Our Train struck of 30·5·19 - Spent a Couch on Leave	
			to WK. No 3 Coy Capt. W G Best of Concentration Camp 6 WK for registration.	
	31		No 1 Coy 1 O R admitted Hospital. No 2 Coy 20 R on leave 6 WK.	

O Hill
Lieut Colonel
Commanding Southern Rwl Train

Southern Div'l Train. page 9.

WAR DIARY
INTELLIGENCE SUMMARY
(Erase heading not required.)

Army Form C. 2118.

VOL I

Place	Date 1919	Hour	Summary of Events and Information	Remarks and references to Appendices
Odenthal	June 1		No. 2 Coy. 1 OR leave to UK. 4 Coy. 1 OR discharged from Hospital.	
	2		No. 1 Coy. 2 OR on leave to UK. 1 OR admitted to Hospital. 10 OR to UK for demobilization 2 Coy 20R	
			to UK for demobilization. No. 3 Coy. 5 OR to UK for demobilization. 3 OR on leave to UK.	
			No. 4 Coy. 7 OR to UK for demobilization. 1 OR on leave to UK. 2 heer. J.L. Hurford	
			joined from 1 Army Aux (Horse) Coy. Lieut Hurford J. on leave to UK	
	3		No. 1 Coy. 1 OR on leave to UK. 1 OR discharged from Hospital. No. 4 Coy. 10 SM carbs. from 88 Field Amb.	
	4		No. 1 Coy. 1 OR on leave to UK.	
	6		No. 4 Coy. 1 OR on leave to UK	
	7		No. 1 Coy. 1 OR admitted to Hospital. No. 2 Coy. 2 OR on leave to UK. No. 3 Coy. 2 OR on	
			leave to UK.	
	8		No. 3 Coy. 3 OR on leave to UK. No. 4 Coy. 2 OR on leave to UK.	
	9		No. 1 Coy. 12 OR to UK for demobilization. 1 OR from Hospital. 1/Capt A.R.T Jennings on	
			leave to UK. No. 2 Coy. 4 OR to UK for demobilization. No. 3 Coy. 6 OR to UK for demobilization	
			1 OR on leave to UK. No. 4 Coy. 5 OR to UK. 5 OR to UK for demobilization. 2 OR on leave to UK	
	10		No. 1 Coy. 1 OR on leave to UK. No. 2 Coy. 2 OR on leave to UK. No. 3 Coy. 1 OR on leave to UK.	
	11		No. 1 Coy. 3 OR on leave to UK. No. 2 Coy. 2 OR on leave to UK.	

VOL I WAR DIARY Southern Div¹ Train Army Form C. 2118.
or
INTELLIGENCE SUMMARY
(Erase heading not required.)

Page 10.

Place	Date 1919	Hour	Summary of Events and Information	Remarks and references to Appendices
Odenthal	June 12		No 1 Coy. 7 LIEUT AUSTIN HOLLOWELL HARDY. R.A.S.C. joined from No 1 Div¹ Train Hdqrs. On strength as from 10th inst. 1 OR admitted to Hospital No 1 by 1 no 2 have evacuated to No 2 Vet. Hospl.	
	13		No 1 Coy. 2 OR admitted to Hospital	
	14		No 1 Coy. 1 OR transferred to cadre establishment of 89th Field Ambulance.	
	15		No 1 Coy. 1 OR discharged from hospital.	
	16		No 1 Coy. 19 OR to UK for demobilisation. No 2 Coy. 12 OR to UK for demobilisation. No 3 Coy 4 OR to UK for demobilisation No 4 Coy. 6 OR to UK for demobilisation.	
	17		No casualties.	
	18		No 1 Coy. 1 OR discharged from Hospital. Supplies for Div¹ Troops group drawn by H.T. from Railhead BERG GLADBACH. Supplies for 1st Southern Brigade group drawn by M.T. from Railhead BERG GLADBACH.	
	19		Supplies for 2nd & 3rd Southern Brigade groups drawn by M.T. from railhead BURSCHEID. Supply wagons march loaded with Units defiled on arrival in new area. Refilling for Div¹ Troops group BERG GLADBACH. No 1 South. Brigade group KALTENHERBURG. No 2 South. Brigade group SOLINGEN. No 3 South. Brigade group BURG.	

VOL I WAR DIARY Southern Div. Train

INTELLIGENCE SUMMARY

PAGE 11

Place	Date 1919	Hour	Summary of Events and Information	Remarks and references to Appendices
ODENTHAL	June 19		Continued. — No 1 Coy 1 OR discharged from Hospital. No 3 Coy 1 HD horse died	
	20		No 2 Coy moved to BURSCHEID No 3 Coy to SOLINGEN No 4 Coy to BURG. Refilling party refreshing remained the same. No 1 South Pole front supplies drawn by HT No 1 Coy 12 HD horses tampling 26 24 Vet Hospital. No 4 Coy 1 OR admitted to Hospital	
	21		Supplies renewed the same.	
	22		— ditto —	
	23		— ditto — No 1 Coy 10 OR b/UK for demobilisation 1 OR b/UK for home Establishment No 2 Coy 20 R b/UK for demobilisation. No 3 Coy 6 OR b/UK for demobilisation No 4 Coy 1 OR b/UK for demobilisation	
	24		— ditto — No 1 Coy 1 OR b/UK for demobilisation	
	25		— ditto — No 1 Coy 1 OR admitted to Hospital.	
	26		— ditto — No 4 Coy 1 OR evacuated to Hospital	
	27		— ditto — No 1 Coy 1 OR admitted to Hospital.	
	28		— ditto —	
	29		— ditto — Lt Col OR. I. HULLS on leave to UK. No 1 Coy 1 OR on leave to UK. No 3 Coy 1 OR to UK for demobilisation	

PAGE 12.

WAR DIARY SOUTHERN DIVISIONAL TRAIN
VOL. I INTELLIGENCE SUMMARY

Place	Date	Hour	Summary of Events and Information	Remarks and references to Appendices
ODENTHAL	Jan 20 1919		Supplies as for 29th inst. of No 1 Coy. 1CR discharged from Hospital to 10 R.B.W.R. for demobilization. No 2 Coy. 4 OR B.W.R. for demobilization. No 3 Coy 20 R.B.W.R. for demobilization. No 4 Coy. 6 OR B.W.R. for demobilization. 1 OR on leave B.W.R.	

A Beecroft
Major
Commanding Southern Div'l Train R.A.S.C.

PAGE 13

VOL I

Northern Divl Train

WAR DIARY
INTELLIGENCE SUMMARY
(Erase heading not required.)

Army Form C. 2118.

Place	Date 1919	Hour	Summary of Events and Information	Remarks and references to Appendices
ODENTHAL	July 1		Units of Divison prepared Review Formguard breakfasts No 2 Coy. 1 OR on leave to U.K.	
	2		No 3 Company moved from SOLINGEN to BURSCHEID No 2 Company moved from BURSCHEID to BERG GLADBACH No 4 Company from BURG to WERMELSKIRCHEN	
			Supply wagons marched loaded with Units to follow on completion of move	
			Supplies drawn from Cullied by M.T.	
			No 1 Coy. 1 OR on leave to U.K. 12 OR to U.K. for demobilisation No 4 Coy. 2 OR on leave to U.K.	
	3		Supplies drawn from Cullied by H.T. except above Company Supply drawn by M.T.	
			127 Battery R.G.A. transferred to II Corps Troops for Supplies	
			No 1 Coy. 1 OR on leave to U.K. 2 OR to U.K. for demobilisation. No 2 Company 1 OR to U.K. for demob.	
			No 3 Coy. 4 OR to U.K. for demob.	
	4		Supplies drawn by H.T. from Cullied No 1 Coy. 2 OR 20 R from 29 M.G. Bn taken on strength	
			1 OR on leave to U.K. 5 OR to U.K. for demobilisation CAPT R.C.O. VIVEASH R.A.S.C. on leave to U.K. No 3 Coy. 2 OR on leave to U.K. No 4 Coy. 2 OR on leave to U.K.	
	5		No 4 Coy. 1 OR on leave to U.K.	
	6		No casualties	

PAGE 14

Army Form C. 2118.

WAR DIARY
of Southern Rail Train
INTELLIGENCE SUMMARY.
(Erase heading not required.)

Place	Date	Hour	Summary of Events and Information	Remarks and references to Appendices
ODENTHAL	July 7		No 1 Coy. 1 OR attached admitted to Hospital.	
	8		No 4 Coy. 8 OR U.K. for demobilization	
	9		No 2 Coy. 1 OR U.K. for demobilization	
	10		No 1 Coy. 1 OR admitted to Hospital	
	13		No 1 Coy. 1 OR on leave 2 OR U.K. for demobilization	
	14		No 1 Coy. 1 OR admitted to Hospital 2 OR U.K. for demob 3 OR U.K. for demobilization No 3 Coy. 1 OR U.K for demobilization No 2 Coy 7 LIEUT	
			H. JEANS R.A.S.C. to U.K. for demobilization No 3 Coy. 1 OR U.K. on leave to U.K.	
	15		No 2 Coy. 1 L/Dhorse to 18th MVS No 3 Coy 1 OR U.K. for demobilization	
	16		No 3 Coy 1 HD have evacuated to 18 MVS	
	17		No 1 Coy. 1 OR discharged from Hospital.	
	18		No 1 Coy. 1 OR discharged from Hospital. 2 Coy. 1 OR admitted to Hospital	
	19		No 1 Coy. MAJOR C & BEECROFT on leave U.K. No 2 Coy. 1 OR U.K. for demob. LIEUT HURFORD admitted to Hospital	
	20		No 1 Coy. 5 OR U.K. for demobilization	
	21		No 4 Coy 2 OR U.K. for demobilization	
	23		No 2 Coy. 3 OR U.K. for demob. No 3 Coy. 1 OR U.K. for demobilization	

July. PAGE 15. Army Form C. 2118.

WAR DIARY
or
INTELLIGENCE SUMMARY.   Southern Rail Train

(Erase heading not required.)

Place	Date	Hour	Summary of Events and Information	Remarks and references to Appendices
ODENTHAL	July		No 1 Coy 6 ORs RWK for demobilization. No 2 Coy 1 OR KWK for demob.	
	25		No 4 Coy 1 OR WWK for demob.	
	26		No 4 Coy 1 OR WWK for demob.	
	27		2 Riding horses #21 HD "E" horses Remount Depot Cologne	
			No 1 Coy 1 OR discharged from hospital. No 2 Coy 1 OR evacuated sick 15 UK.	
			LIEUT T S BRAGG E GIRDLE to UK for demob	
	29		No 1 Coy 1 OR RWK for demob. No 2 Coy 1 OR KWK for demob.	
	30		No 1 Coy 1 OR on leave UK	
	31		No 1 Coy 5 ORs WK for demobilization. No 2 Coy 1 OR WK for demob	

W Hill Lt Colonel
Commanding Southern Rail Train

PAGE 16

August 1919

WAR DIARY

INTELLIGENCE SUMMARY Southern Rwt Train

VOL. I

Army Form C. 2118.

Place	Date	Hour	Summary of Events and Information	Remarks and references to Appendices
ODENTHAL	Aug 3		No 1 Coy 1 OR Readmitted to Hospital. 1 OR on Leave B/UK 1 OR B/UK for demobilisation	
			No 1 Coy 1 OR B/UK for demobilisation 24 OR Infantry Transferred to K/ASC on 25/7/19	
			No 3 Coy 1 OR B/UK for demobilisation 50 OR Infantry transferred to K/ASC	
			No 4 Coy 1 OR discharged from Hospital	
	7		No 1 Coy 1 OR on Leave B/UK No 2 Coy 1 OR on Leave B/UK No 1 Coy 47 OR Infantry transferred K/ASC	
	6		No 1 Coy 1 OR discharged from Hosp. 1 OR Leave B/UK 2 Coy 1 OR on Leave B/UK 1 OR to Coy	
			The LIEUT RIDE AT Transferred from Light Armoured Train 3/8/19	
	7		No 1 Coy 1 OR B/UK for demobilisation	
	8		No 1 Coy 2 OR on Leave B/UK 1 OR discharged from Hospital	
	9		No 1 Coy 1 HD Base 6/8 M.V.S.	
	10		6 HD 1st Riding Horses marked 'S' evacuated to high ed. over Sale Ring Solingen	
	11		No 1 Coy 1 OR on Leave B/UK 2 Coy 2 OR on Leave B/UK No 3 Coy CAPT SHADWELL Capt. B/UK	
	12		No 2 Coy 1 Riding Horse to 18 M.V.S	
	13		No 1 Coy 1 OR on Leave B/UK No 2 Coy 1 OR admitted to Hospital	
	14		No 2 Coy 1 OR on Leave B/UK 1 OR Infantry transferred K/ASC LIEUT S. H. HEARD attached proceeded to Base Supply Depot ANTWERP	

• PAGE 17 •

August 1919 — WAR DIARY Southern Div¹ Train — Army Form C. 2118.

INTELLIGENCE SUMMARY. VOL I

Place	Date	Hour	Summary of Events and Information	Remarks and references to Appendices
ODENTHAL	Aug 15		No 1 Coy 1HD horse to C.E.S. No 2 Coy 1MR Leave B/UK of No 3 Coy 10R admitted to Hospital	
	16		No 1 Coy 10R/UK for demobilization. of No 2 Coy 10R leave B/UK	
	17		No 1 Coy 2 OR admitted to Hospital 2 Coy 1MR leave B/UK	
	18		No 1 Coy 1OR discharged from hospital No 3 Coy CAPT L J L SPARKER leave to PARIS	
			No 4 Coy LIEUT A FORBES on leave B/UK	
	19		No 3 Coy 2 Riding Horses from Rhine Army Remount Depot	
	20		No 3 Coy 1MR Infantry transferred to R A S C	
	21		LIEUT JAMES J A on leave B/UK	
	22		MAJOR W H PRESTON RASC 14 Days leave to U.K. 1OR from 18 M.V.S 1 Horse from 18 M.V.S	
	23		8 OR to Concentration Camp for demobilisation. 1HD & 18 MVS 1 Riding Station from 4 C⁹	
	24		1OR to HP 1 Taken from MIDLAND DIV TRAIN	
	25/26		1 Rider to No 8 Veterinary HP	
	27		2/LIEUT P C CORNWALL RASC leave to U.K 1OR leave to U K 1 HD 14	
	28		1 Stolen rider returned by Police 1 OR to Concentration Camp for demobilisation	
	29		1OR to HP 1 OR from HP LIEUT W PORTEOUS RASC leave to UK	
	30/31		1 OR 4 HP	

W⁰ G Salfe Lt/14 Adjt
Southern Div¹ Train

Southern Div? Train
Army form C. 2118.
225

WAR DIARY
INTELLIGENCE SUMMARY
(Erase heading not required.)

Vol I   15 Oct? PAGE 18

Place	Date	Hour	Summary of Events and Information	Remarks and references to Appendices
ODENTHAL	Sept? 1919	1	1/Lieut N. FASTER R.A.S.C. ADJT MIDLAND DIV TRAIN. Posted for duty as ADJUTANT. Southern Div Train. 1 O/R from Southern Div Train posted to No 1 Coy. 1 O/R Leave to UK. 1 O/R transferred from 226 Emp? Coy as a Driver	W.T.
		2	1 O/R " " "	
		3/4	1st Lieut A. FORBES, R.A.S.C. 14 days leave to UK. 1 O/R to HP. 1 O/R from HP. Lt J.A. James from Leave	
		5	2 O/R Leave to UK. LIEUT A.T. TRIDEL R.A.S.C. Leave to UK	
		6	1 O/R Leave to UK. MAJOR W.H. PRESTON R.A.S.C. from leave to UK	
		7	No Entry	
		8	CAPT W. CAMPBELL R.A.S.C. Leave to UK. 1 O/R Leave to UK. 1 O/R to HP. 5 O/R to Demobilisation Camp for DEMOB.	
		9	1 O/R Leave to UK. 1 O/R to HP.	
		10	1 O/R Leave to UK. 1 O/R to HP.	
		11	Lieut H. PORTEOUS R.A.S.C. from leave to UK. 1 O/R leave to UK. 1 O/R from 8th F.AMB.	
		12	1 O/R leave to UK. 3 O/R from 82 M.T. RECEPTION PARK WISSANT. 2 O/R from HP.	
		13	LIEUT J.A JAMES. R.A.S.C. to 62 M.T.Reception Park. Wissant 1 O/R leave UK. 1 O/R to HP.	
		14	1 O/R Leave to UK.	
		15	1 O/R " " " 2 O/R from HP.	
		16	1 O/R " " " 1 O/R to HP.	
		17	1 O/R " " "	

WAR DIARY Southern Rail Train

INTELLIGENCE SUMMARY
(Erase heading not required.)

Army Form C. 2118.

Vol 1. PAGE 19

Place	Date	Hour	Summary of Events and Information	Remarks and references to Appendices
ODENTHAL	September 1919			
GERMANY	18		1 O.R. leave to U.K.	M.E.
	19		" " " "	
	20		1 O.R. from H.P.	
	21		Lieut A. CROUCH R.A.S.C. leave to U.K. 1 O.R. leave to U.K. 3 O.R. transferred from Infantry	
	22		1 O.R. leave U.K. 10 O.R. to Concentration Camp for Month 1 O.R. to H.P.	
	23		1 O.R. leave to U.K.	
	24		1 O.R. " " "	
	25/26		The Entries	
	27		20 "T" Horses to REMOUNT DEPÔT. COLOGNE. 1 O.R. to H.P.	
	28		1 O.R. from H.P.	
	29/30		NO ENTRY.	

W. Fisher Capt RASC
Southern Rail Train

Army Form C. 2118.

WAR DIARY or INTELLIGENCE SUMMARY.

(Erase heading not required.)

Southern Div? Train
225-8
VOL-1- PAGE 20

Place	Date	Hour	Summary of Events and Information	Remarks and references to Appendices
ODENTHAL	October 1919			
GERMANY	1		2 O/R from H.P.	18
	2		1 O/R to H.P. 8 Ampith. Journals circulated with 15th B" HANTS at D.I.R. COLOGNE 5 NOV 1919	
	3		1 O/R transferred M.T. Branch to Southern Div. M.T.C° 7/Lieut. A.T. RIDEL R.A.S.C. No 23 M.T. Roughton Park	
	4/5		1 C.S.L. Meyer Capt./S. Howard attached to Rev. H.Q.	
	6		1 O/R to H.P.	
	7		2 · 3 (Sold. Horses) to Divisional Mobile Veterinary Colorque. 4 Ampith. Journals from 15th Hanks. Authorised from 2 D.I.R. Colorque	
	8		161 R.D. M.T.C° 1 N.R.b H.P. 1 H.R. from H.P.	
	9		2 O/R to Reinforcement Overseas College. L.H. Crouch R.A.S.C. from Leave to U.K.	
	10		3 O/R to Consolidation Camps. for Demob. 1 O/R from H.P. 2 H.R. Remounts H.Q. 240 from J.H.Q. 2 O/R here Re-inf. M.T.C°"1	
	11		Capt L.C. Shadwell R.A.S.C. to 42nd M.T. Ros. Ho? ton Park Missant. 1 O/R from H.P. 1 H.R. from H.P.	
	12		8 O/R to Consolidation Camps. for Demob. 1 H.R. from H.P.	
	13		1 O/R from H.P.	
	14		1 O/R to H.P. 1 H.R. back to U.K.	
	15		8 O/R to Rev. M.T.C.s. 3 W.O. Horses & 1 G.S. Wagon from Rept. Regimental Camp. 8 O/R from R.I.K. R O/R to Consolidation Camps for Hospital is alone	
	16		Lieut. J.H. Hurford R.A.S.C. back to U.K. 1 O/R leave to U.K. 8 O/R to Consolidation Camp for Demobilis. U.K	

Army Form C. 2118.

Southern Lines [?] Train

WAR DIARY
or
INTELLIGENCE SUMMARY.
(Erase heading not required.)

Vol. I. Page 21

Instructions regarding War Diaries and Intelligence Summaries are contained in F. S. Regs., Part II. and the Staff Manual respectively. Title pages will be prepared in manuscript.

Place	Date	Hour	Summary of Events and Information	Remarks and references to Appendices
ODENTHAL, GERMANY	Oct/45		12 O/R	12 O/R
	17		8 O/R March to U.K. 8 O/R to Cumberton Camp for Demobilisation	
	18		50/R to Cumberton Camp for Demobilisation	
	19		Capt L.J.L. SPARKE RASC from leave to U.K. 29/R to Cumberton Camp for Demobilisation	
	20		2 O/R March to U.K.	
	21		1 O/R from HP. 1 O/R March to U.K.	
	22		1 KD Horse to MVS. 2 O/R Leave to U.K.	
	23		2 O/R Back to U.K.	
	24		4 KD Horses to MVS. 8 O/R Transferred from Infantry	
	25		1 O/R from HP. "H.D." Horses from 2/4 13th Hrs. S. Capt R.C.O. HYEASH RASC Leave to U.K. 2 O/R Back to U.K.	
	26		50 O/R from Richard Hut Train. 18 Horses from Hudson to RA [?]	
	27		4 O/R to Cumberton Camp for Demobilisation. 2 O/R Back to U.K.	
	28		19 O/R March to U.K. 5 KD Horses from RS. "70 & 71st" L.J.L. SPARKE RASC to U.K. for Demobilisation	
	29		1 O/R to HP. 1 O/R from HP. 11 Horses from Light Hut Train. 11 Horses to 18 M.V.S.	
	30		Capt E. O'TOWER RASC leave to U.K. 10 O/R March to U.K.	
	31		10 O/R March to U.K. 11 O/R from Light Hut Train	

Welshe Cpl. A/Sgt
Southern Hut Train

www.ingramcontent.com/pod-product-compliance
Lightning Source LLC
Chambersburg PA
CBHW081526160426
43191CB00011B/1691